COSMO CONFESSIONS

COSMO CONFESSIONS

Hundreds of Absolutely Shameful, Scandalous, and Sexy Real-Life Tales!

From the Editors of **COSMOPOLITAN**

Hearst Books
A Division of Sterling Publishing Co., Inc.
New York

CONTENTS

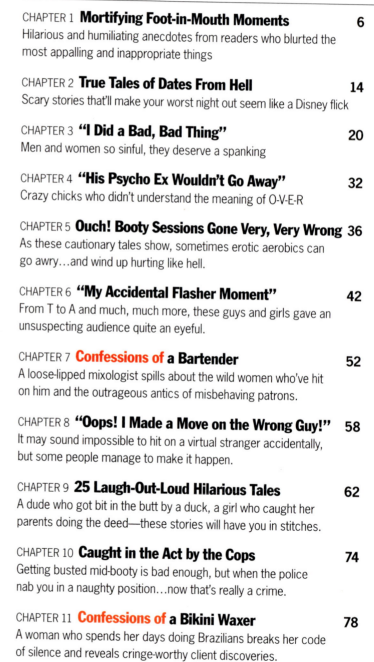

MORTIFYING
FOOT-IN-MOUTH
MOMENTS

Think you've made an embarrassing faux pas? Just wait until you read these hilarious and humiliating anecdotes from readers who blurted the most appalling and inappropriate things. They're still hiding under a rock.

"You're cute, but say one more word and you might ruin your chances."

Size Matters

"One afternoon my friend and I were joking that there should be date insurance that would pay off if your crush turned out to be a psycho or not so well-endowed. The next day we were hanging out when she handed me my cordless phone and said, 'It's your insurance agent.' I hadn't heard it ring and I didn't have an insurance agent, so I assumed she was riffing on our joke from before. I picked it up and said, 'Hello, I'm interested in the big-penis no-fault plan.' My friend blanched, and I suddenly realized the talk light was on but there was no dial tone. I said hello, and there was someone on the line—a friend of my mom's who happened to be an insurance agent. My mother had asked her to call me about coverage for a car I was thinking of buying. I gave her a garbled explanation of our joke and apologized. Fortunately, she had a sense of humor, laughed it off, and gave me a good deal."—*Christie, 27*

Party Pooper

"I had a crush on this girl, Melissa, for months, but every time I tried to talk to her I froze up. One night I ran into her at a party and we started talking about our favorite foods. She mentioned she was a vegan, and when I asked why, she told me she had stomach problems. Before I even knew what I was saying, I started telling her that red meat gave me diarrhea. She was really nice about the whole thing and just smiled and nodded. But when I realized what I'd said, my mouth dropped open and I asked, 'Did I really just say that?' She nodded yes, then politely changed the subject." —*Jon, 24*

If you think these are red, you should have seen her face.

Table Turn-on

"One night my beau and I were at a fancy restaurant. We had shared a bottle of wine, so I was feeling gutsy. I went to the ladies' room, slipped off my red lace panties, and folded them neatly in my hand. When I got back to the table, I passed them to him with a wink. He exclaimed loudly, 'What's this, your underwear?' He didn't have any idea he was broadcasting what I'd done to the entire restaurant. As all eyes turned to us, I wanted to crawl under the table and die." —Kathleen, 26

"Just as the music stopped, I screamed something I didn't want my ex to hear...."

Udder-ly Ridiculous

"My boyfriend brought me to a party in his hometown. I didn't think I'd know anyone there, but I ran into an old friend who happened to have relocated to the town. She was reminding me of this guy I used to date whose mom had the saggiest breasts we'd ever seen. I leaned over and screamed, 'Luckily, my new guy's mom is flat chested, so I don't have to stare at those udders anymore!' Just as the words came out of my mouth, the music went dead, and the lights went out. The whole room heard! When the lights came on again, I explained the story to my guy, who started cracking up and told me not to worry about it." —Kerri, 29

Not-So-True Love

"I was at Oktoberfest in Germany when I met this incredible girl. We spent the whole day together, drinking beer and getting to know each other. I was living in France at the time, and she was just visiting for a few days from the States, so even though there was chemistry, I knew the relationship wouldn't last. At the end of the day we got a hotel room and went at it for hours. The next morning I waited with her on the street while she hailed a cab. I must have still been a bit tipsy because, as her cab pulled away, I yelled out, 'I love you!' Oops! Immediately the cab came to a stop and I thought, *Oh no, what did I say?* She leaped out of the car, jumped on me, and told me she would stay for a week. I didn't know how to let her down, so I spent the entire time being rude and disrespectful to her. After a few days she took off, claiming she didn't see a future for us." —Joe, 25

He drank this and fell for her—sort of.

Don't speak. Just unbutton the rest of your shirt.

✈ First-Class Ass

"A few months ago I was on a late-night flight when I fell asleep. All of a sudden, in the middle of a very dirty dream, the woman in the next seat started shaking me. I woke up to find the entire first-class cabin staring at me. Apparently, I had spent five minutes moaning so loudly that I'd disturbed everyone around me. Finally when I started saying, 'Oh, yeah, baby,' the woman beside me decided it was time to wake me up." —Lee, 26

IN THE HEAT OF THE MOMENT

Why do we end up saying stupid things sometimes? Well, according to Perry Buffington, PhD, author of *Cheap Psychological Tricks for Lovers*, when you're nervous, you get a rush of adrenaline that can cloud your thinking and judgment, causing you to say something you might not have meant to.

Without these on, this chick had X-rated vision.

Out of Sight

"I was at the beach one day checking out my latest crush, Brad. My eyesight is pretty bad, but because I didn't want Brad to see me in my glasses, I went without them. My best friend, Jane, was supposed to meet me there, so I went looking for her. When I saw her at the snack bar, I strolled up, grabbed a piece of her pretzel, and, gazing at my dream dude back on the sand, said, 'Man, is Brad the hottest piece of ass ever or what?' I turned to Jane for her reaction and some woman who was clearly not Jane was staring at me like I had three heads. I stammered out an apology and started to head back to my chair, but the woman grabbed my arm and said, 'I'll be sure to warn my boyfriend, Brad, about a nearsighted crazy woman with a really bad perm!'" —Saundra, 20

"Let's try that again: Does my butt look big in these jeans?"

Lust on the Line

"I work in tech support at an Internet-service company and, as a joke, my girl would sometimes call in and talk about all the X-rated things she wanted to do to me. One afternoon I returned from lunch, and a coworker said my girlfriend was on hold for me. I picked up the phone and whispered, 'Does this naughty woman want a spanking?' The line went quiet, then I heard, 'This is your boss. Come to my office now.' I walked in and explained that I'd picked up the wrong extension. My boss didn't fire me, but I was barred from phone duty." —Neil, 21

"I picked up the phone and whispered, 'Does this naughty woman want a spanking?'"

YOU GO, GIRL!

You've gotta give this chick credit: She's got balls.

Foul Play

"I was at a bar when I saw a gorgeous guy sitting across the room. I coyly glanced at him, and eventually he and some of his buds came over. After about five minutes, I realized they were total sports fanatics. I'm clueless when it comes to that stuff, but I wanted to impress them, so I lied and said I was a huge Yankees fan. The cute guy got really excited and asked me if I had been to any games. I didn't want to disappoint him, so I nodded and replied, 'Sure. The last baseball game I went to was when the Mets played the Yankees in the Super Bowl.' My hottie gave me a disgusted look and said, 'Uh…you mean the World Series.' Everyone laughed and then walked away." —Maureen, 33

(top to bottom, from left) ANNA PALMA. JACK MISKELL. Photographer's Choice/Getty Images. JACK MISKELL.

Ball Buster

"Last summer I was on the phone with a boy I liked when we started talking about swing dancing. Eventually the conversation progressed until we were discussing how much fun old-school dancing could be. He then mentioned that he'd always wanted to learn how to ballroom dance, and I exclaimed, 'Oh, I love balls!' This was followed by a really awkward silence until he did an 'Uh, anyway…' and moved on." —Annie, 24

Pantie Rage

"I started seeing this girl, Deb, even though I was still sleeping with my ex. One afternoon Deb was over while I did the laundry. I noticed that a pair of lacy red panties had made it in with my stuff, so without thinking, I handed them to her and said, 'Here are those panties I love so much on you.' Deb looked like she wanted to kill me. She screamed, 'Next time you're having sex with two girls at once, don't mix up their underwear!' Then she threw the panties in my face and stormed out." —Ryan, 32

Just one more reason to hire a cleaning lady.

This dude's *so* in the doghouse.

Bad Dog

"I had been dating Jackie for a few months when she stopped taking my calls. I found out that she had been going out with another guy the entire time she was with me. Weeks went by, and then one night I saw Jackie out at a bar with this older man. To get back at her I walked over and said, 'Hey, she loves to do it doggie-style.' They both turned to me in shock, and the man yelled, 'You're sick! She's my daughter!' " —Jesse, 22

"I handed the panties to my girlfriend and said, 'Here's the pair I love.' She looked like she wanted to kill me!"

Cringe-Worthy Complaint

"My friends and I stopped for food at this roadside diner. Our server was really awkward and kept screwing up. He never brought us silverware, mixed up the orders, and forgot about my friend's meal completely. I'd never had such bad service in my life. I was at my wit's end, so I lost it and started screaming at him in front of the whole restaurant, 'What are you, some kind of idiot?' A minute later the manager came running over to the table. I thought she was going to fire the waiter, but instead she looked at me like I was the devil and said, 'Gil is my son, and he's mentally retarded. Do you usually speak to the disabled that way?' Ashamed, we paid our bill and hightailed it out of there." —Claire, 31

1

OOPS! Parent Trap

"I was on a date with this guy, Alex, and things were going really well. He was good-looking and had a great job. I really thought I could have a future with this guy. At one point, we got on the topic of terrible first dates, so I started telling him about this one guy I went out with who was 30 years old and still lived at home with his parents. I was going on about what a twisted loser this guy was when Alex's face dropped. He then told me that he had moved home a few months before because his mom was very sick and needed 24-hour care. I never felt so badly in my whole life. Needless to say, there was no second date." —*Janet, 23*

"I walked up to the counter in my itty-bitty dress and said to my hunky vet, 'I came here to get Lucky....' "

Tongue Twisted

"My girlfriend and I were walking through the park and feeling silly. We were taking sentences and switching around the words to create naughty phrases. At one point, we walked up to a vendor who asked if we'd like a hot dog. My girlfriend turned to me and said, 'I'll make your dog hot!' and we burst out laughing. Then a little girl came up and asked for a cherry Popsicle, and I said, 'I'll pop your cherry!' When I realized what I'd said I felt horrible, but I wasn't nearly as upset as the girl's mother." —*Andrew, 23*

Forget your foot—stick this in your mouth.

A Cut Above

"I was spending a semester in London and started dating a local guy. One afternoon he invited me over to his parents' house for tea. I was really nervous because I'd never been in a proper British home. As it turned out, they were great people, and we were really hitting it off— that is, until his mother asked me if there was anything different about dating a man from the U.K. I could have mentioned the English manners or adorable accent, but instead I told her the only difference was that most American guys were circumcised. Yep, that was the last time I was invited over." —*Nancy, 23*

Animal Urges

"I was taking my kitten Lucky to the doctor every chance I had because my vet is so hot. Once, when I came by to pick up my cat after he'd had a special skin treatment, I made sure to wear a supersexy outfit. I walked up to the counter in my itty-bitty dress, saw my hunky vet, and blurted out, 'I'm here to get Lucky.' When it dawned on me how it sounded, I blushed. The vet just smiled and said all he could help me with was my pet." —*Elana, 24*

"I goofed and sent an e-mail to my boss speculating about her weight loss!"

Some advice: Never leave the house again.

Diet Joke

"One summer the president of our company took a month off. When she came back, she was about 40 pounds lighter, which got the office gossips buzzing. Everyone had her own theory as to how she'd lost the weight, ranging from liposuction to a parasite. One afternoon a coworker and I were e-mailing, coming up with our own crazy ideas. I hit reply on an e-mail and wrote, 'Ms. Walker is still too flabby to have had lipo, so I think it was stomach stapling.' Twenty minutes later I got an e-mail from Ms. Walker: 'Actually, I went on a no-carb diet while on vacation. You might want to try it yourself.' Apparently I had responded to the wrong e-mail!"

—Mary Anne, 31

THE WORST THINGS YOU COULD SAY TO...

If you really want to ruin a relationship, try one of these rude lines:

THE VICTIM	THE CRIMINAL COMMENT
Your best friend	"Yeah, your boyfriend really *is* great in bed."
Your new guy	"That's it? But your hands and feet are so big!"
Your boyfriend's mom	"Geez, when's the last time you redecorated? '78?"
Your boss	"I'm on the phone with my boyfriend. Can it wait a sec?"
Your parents	"I'll need years of therapy to fix all the mistakes you made."

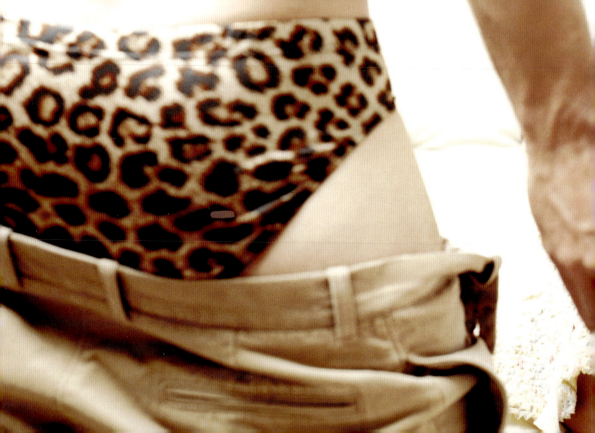

TRUE TALES OF DATES FROM HELL

When you're single, sucky first dates are par for the course. But after reading these scary stories, even your worst night out will seem like a Disney flick.

"I was hoping he'd be an animal in the sack, but this is not what I had in mind."

Romeo With a Restraining Order

"On our first date, Aaron suggested we go for a drive after we'd seen a movie. I thought it would be a good chance for us to casually shoot the breeze and get to know each other better. But he wouldn't respond to small talk—he just cruised around a certain block about three times, pausing in front of one house in particular. I was a little concerned and asked him what was up. In a forced relaxed tone he said, 'My ex lives there, and I want to see if she's home right now.' I was weirded out and asked him to take me back to my apartment. He agreed, but spent the rest of the ride asking if I would vouch that he had not verbally harassed his ex if she sent the cops to question him. I couldn't get out of the car fast enough. What a freak!" —Angie, 24

Call of the Wild

"One night after being out with this guy, I went back to his house. We were smooching on the sofa, and as things got more intense, he started making these weird ape sounds. At first I just thought that the noises were his bizarre version of moaning, but then he began beating his chest and asking me to make monkey noises too. He said he'd always wondered what it would be like to make love to an ape woman. Um, can you say psycho? As soon as I heard that, I quickly threw on my clothes and told him to find some other girl to fulfill his creepy Tarzan-and-Jane fantasy." —Leigh, 25

There's no room for three.

Creature Feature

"I was dating a grad student who worked at a research lab. He was geeky, but he was also really hot. One night, he invited me over to hang out. After watching a flick, we retreated to the bedroom for a little action. A few minutes after we started messing around, I felt something crawling on me. I screamed and jumped out of bed. As it turned out, he'd taken a few mice home from the lab and had accidentally left the top off their cage. A couple of them had found their way underneath the comforter and onto me. I was so freaked out that I refused to spend the night."

—Lacey, 26

Bite Me

"On our second date, Will was waiting at the bar of the restaurant when I arrived. I was on time, but he had already downed a highball and was nursing another. I told him I'd like a ginger ale and went to see when the table would be ready. When I got back, he had a drink waiting for me. I took a sip, and found it obviously had been spiked with a hearty dose of vodka. I asked why he'd ordered me an alcoholic drink, and he slurred, 'I'd like you to be drunk before we eat.' Then he leaned closer to me and whispered, 'You have beautiful bite-size boobies.' I almost fell off my chair! As soon as I recovered I said, 'I suddenly feel sick, and I'm leaving.' On my way out he yelled after me, but I just kept on going."

—Kelly, 29

"He leaned in closer to me and whispered something that almost made me fall off my chair...."

Cheap Date

"My friends set me up with this dude they swore was great. He chose a nice restaurant, which I took as a good sign, but then he ordered us both tap water and suggested we split a salad and an entrée. He made loud references to the cost of things: Looking at the menu he joked, 'Are these prices in pesos?' I could tell the restaurant staff was snickering at us. When the food came he said, 'You'd think the portions would be as big as the table for what we're paying!' But that was nothing compared to the moment at the end of the meal when he whispered, 'Is your napkin clean?' Puzzled, I replied that it was and he said, 'Give it to me.' He then folded up our leftover bread in the napkins and put them in his jacket pocket. Noticing my stunned look he said, 'Quit glaring, will you? I'm just trying to get my money's worth from this place.'" *—Hannah, 23*

This thing hasn't been opened since '91.

"You can try all you want, but this date is officially over."

Send out the Clown

"I was totally into this guy I was dating—until he invited me back to his place for the first time. I looked around to find it decorated in a clown motif. He had clown dolls on the shelves, several clown posters on the walls, and even a clown puppet on his bed. It was creepy, but I thought there might be a good reason for it. When I asked him why he was so into clowns, he didn't give an answer. Instead, he pulled a clown costume out of his closet and asked if I wanted him to put it on. I looked at him, confused, and he said, 'Come on, it's sexy.' I told him I wasn't feeling well and left before I had to watch him juggle." —*Alexis, 24*

Breast Exam

"During my senior year of college I went on a few dates with Tom, who was a third-year medical student. On our second date, we went to dinner and then back to his apartment to hang out and talk. In the middle of our make-out session, Tom told me he had a practical exam the next day and asked if he could listen to my heart for practice. I had all of my clothes on at this point, and he said he needed me to take off my shirt for his trial run. I felt comfortable with him, so I took it off and let him 'listen to my heart.' After a while, it became obvious that all Tom was really doing was groping me with his stethoscope. I was so weirded out that I grabbed my shirt and hightailed it out of there. Before walking out the door, I looked back and said, 'All you had to do was ask!'" —*Lindel, 27*

Nothing But the Tooth

"After months of subtle flirting in the office, my hot male coworker asked me out on a date. I was so excited, because even though our interactions had been mostly work-related, I thought we had a strong connection. The night of the date, we went to a funky diner near my place. I kept thinking how cute he was, but when our server brought over the food, he stopped midsentence and said, 'Oh yeah, I forgot to tell you. I have to take out my fake tooth when I eat!' He then pulled out his front tooth, placed it on a napkin near his plate, and flashed me a big goofy smile." —*Bertha, 30*

27% **OF WOMEN HAVE BAILED HALFWAY THROUGH A DATE.**

Doctor Doodle-a-Little

"For my third date with this yummy plastic surgeon, I asked him over for dinner. We were having cocktails when he began telling me that I was really beautiful. I was flattered, that is, until he said I'd be more attractive if I 'added some oomph' to my breasts and got rid of the 'excess baggage' on my thighs. I was wearing a micromini, so he picked up a marker and started circling the areas on my thighs that needed work! I was so insulted that I told him he should consider a lobotomy to make *himself* more attractive, then I showed him to the door." —*Angie, 23*

South-of-the-Border Bummer

"Last year I went on a trip to Mexico with my mom. When we got to our resort, I met this handsome Spanish guy, and we made plans to go out that night. After my mom was asleep, I snuck out of our room and met up with him. We went to a disco together, and then had some fun on the beach under the stars. As we were walking back to the resort, he said he wanted to get me a souvenir. I thought that was sweet until he said that he didn't want his *fiancée* to see him buying it. So instead, he handed me $40 and made reference to the fact that it looked like I needed it. I felt as if I'd just been paid for a one-night stand." —*Mandy, 19*

HOW TO...

BAIL ON A BAD DATE

These tips will help you plot your exit strategy:

Lie Right Away

If you can tell the guy's a chump from the second you sit down, fake a frenzied state immediately. Then tell him that you got an urgent phone call on your way to meet him and unfortunately you can only stay for a drink.

Set Up a Rescue Ring

Before you leave home, discuss an SOS code with a friend. If you text her with the letter "H" for help, that's her cue to call you with a "dire emergency." That way, if things take an ugly turn at any point, your pal can save you.

Be Blunt

If you realize halfway through the date that the two of you aren't clicking, admit as much up front. Try something like, "Listen, I've enjoyed meeting you, but I don't think we're meant to be. I'm going to call it a night."

Run

If Mr. Wrong gets rude, screw tact—you don't have to take it from a guy you barely know. Mumble whatever four-letter words you like in his general direction and head out the door.

SOURCE: JOY DAVIDSON, PHD, AUTHOR OF *FEARLESS SEX: A BABE'S GUIDE TO OVERCOMING ROMANTIC OBSESSIONS AND GETTING THE SEX LIFE YOU DESERVE*

This slimy dude really got burned.

She learned a new meaning to the words *animal attraction*.

2

Putting His Foot in It

"I went out to dinner with this guy who kept making sexual innuendos. When I asked him what he was going to eat, he looked me up and down and said, 'Hopefully, you.' When I asked what he liked to do for fun, he licked his lips and said, 'I'll have to show you.' He turned everything into a come-on. Over dessert he said, 'You look like a naughty girl who'd do bad things to me.' That's when I walked out…spilling my coffee in his lap on the way." —*Paige, 25*

"We went into a stable and were making out when he made the strangest request…."

Tiny-Tool Fool

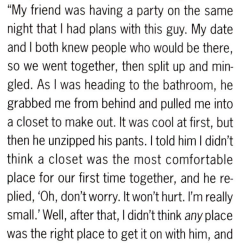

EWWW!

"My friend was having a party on the same night that I had plans with this guy. My date and I both knew people who would be there, so we went together, then split up and mingled. As I was heading to the bathroom, he grabbed me from behind and pulled me into a closet to make out. It was cool at first, but then he unzipped his pants. I told him I didn't think a closet was the most comfortable place for our first time together, and he replied, 'Oh, don't worry. It won't hurt. I'm really small.' Well, after that, I didn't think *any* place was the right place to get it on with him, and I broke things off pronto." —*Courtney, 26*

Diss Jockey

"One day this hunky horseback-riding instructor I was dating offered me a free riding lesson, so we went to the stables after they closed to the public. Later, we walked into an empty stall and started going at it. Suddenly he stopped and asked if I would wear the bridle, which goes in the horse's mouth and is used to steer. I was so disgusted that I mumbled a reason I had to go, then bolted. I never returned his phone calls again!" —*Vanessa, 22*

HAVE YOU EVER MADE UP AN EXCUSE TO GET OUT OF A DATE?

83% OF WOMEN SAID YES.

70% OF GUYS SAID YES.

You don't even want to know the dastardly things she did to get this guy.

"I DID A BAD, **BAD** THING"

There's naughty, and then there's downright evil. These men and women were so sinful, they deserve a serious spanking.

Forrest Hump

"I used to work at a stationery store with a guy who I thought was socially inept. Tom had a bit of a speech impediment and wasn't exactly a genius, but he was sweet and had a crush on me. One night, a few friends and I were out drinking at happy hour and started talking about how easy it is for a woman to get laid. We made a pact that we would all hook up that night, and since our egos were on the line, we gave it our best effort. After a couple of hours at the bar, everyone had managed to find a guy except for me. I refused to face the humiliation, so I called up Tom at the store and begged him to meet us. The sex was awful, but, of course, I called my friends on my cell from his bathroom to tell them how amazing it was. The next morning, I woke up to Tom's mother dragging me out of bed. As it turned out, Tom wasn't socially inept…he was mentally handicapped!" —Lori, 19

Devious Daughter

"A few months ago, my mom went out of town to visit relatives. I couldn't go with her, but I agreed to house-sit while she was gone. One day, her boyfriend Rick came by to pick up some clothes he had left there. He was a little flirty, but I brushed it off—he was dating my mother, after all! But the following night, he came back with a pizza. After having dinner and a couple of margaritas, he kissed me. I knew it was wrong, but it felt so good that I couldn't say no. We ended up spending the night together. I never knew older men could have such stamina. Afterward, we promised never to talk about it again. My mom still has no idea." —Deirdre, 24

Parlez vous…"I don't like you?"

French Diss-Connection

"I was dating this girl who was starting to get way too serious. I wasn't sure how to break it off until I was asked to go on a business trip to France. When I casually mentioned it to Cheryl, she got upset, thinking I was leaving for good. Rather than correct her, I decided to pretend I was moving there, and we ended things. About a week later, when I'd come back from my short trip, I went to get coffee in my neighborhood. When I walked into the place, I saw her sitting across the room. I tried to sneak out, but we made eye contact. She got a huge smile on her face until she saw the look of fear on mine and realized that I hadn't really moved to France after all. I thought she was going to come over and attack me, but, thankfully, she let me leave without making a scene." —Bob, 28

Blind Date Brush-Off

"After my friend's wife nagged me for months, I finally agreed to go on a blind date with her coworker Charlotte, who told me she'd be wearing a red coat. Around seven o'clock, in walked a butt-ugly woman in a red blazer. As soon as I laid eyes on her, I knew I had to take drastic measures. Charlotte came over and said, 'Jared?' I gave her a puzzled look and said, 'My name's Greg.' Realizing I was

"As soon as I laid eyes on the butt-ugly chick they fixed me up with, I knew I had to take drastic measures…."

safe, I decided to buy her a drink and talk to her for a bit. The next morning, I got a tongue-lashing from my friend's wife for standing Charlotte up. But she said it wasn't a complete loss since Charlotte had said she met someone else that night." —Jared, 32

CLEVER QUIPS FOR COMMON CRIMES

Next time you're caught being bad, save face with one of these quick comebacks.

THE CRIME	THE COMEBACK
Cheating	"Baby, I was just learning some tricks to use on you later."
Revenge	"I did it because I love you! Is that such a crime?"
Lying	"Do you need your hearing checked? You misunderstood me."
Talking smack	"Nooooo, I meant the *other* Susie."

Setup Sabotage

"My friend Michelle wanted to set up her friend Brad with my best bud, Lisa. To facilitate the meeting, a group of us made plans to go out for drinks after work one night. I thought Brad was cute, so I was kind of peeved that he was getting hooked up with Lisa. That afternoon, I realized that if I somehow tricked her into not going, then I could weasel my way into Brad's affection. So I called her and told her that I heard a mutual friend was having a major crisis and needed consoling. She skipped the setup to go spend time with our friend, who wasn't exactly ailing. When Lisa eventually figured out my plan, she was mad as hell and hasn't spoken to me since."

—Rose, 32

Moving Ouch

"Every time I tried to break up with my girlfriend Angie, she would freak out. So one day while she was at work, I packed all of her clothes and toiletries in boxes and put them in the front yard along with her furniture. I also changed the locks and left a note on the door that read, 'Angie: Things just aren't working out. Sorry, Dan.' That afternoon, my buddies and I took off on a camping trip so I wouldn't have to deal with her when she came home. Three days later, I returned to find two windows smashed and 20 irate messages from Angie on my voice mail." —Dan, 31

3

Sure he's cute, but he's also a cat killer.

Kitty Splat

"Last summer, my girlfriend went out of town and asked me to look after her three cats, which she loved like children. Well, I accidentally left the garage door open a crack, one of them got out, and I ended up backing over it in the driveway. I was completely freaked out, so I scooped it up and threw it in the neighbors' trash can. When my girlfriend got back, I told her that I had seen the neighbors' teenage son run over her poor cat with his car. She proceeded to sob hysterically on my shoulder, and I comforted her the best I could. Almost a year later, she still won't talk to the neighbors, and they have no idea why." —Brian, 27

Climb into bed with her, and the claws might come out.

Coat Chick

"My office has a big closet where we all leave our coats. One day, I saw my coworker Jill wearing the coolest suede jacket. Jill is stylish and beautiful, with a hot, rich boyfriend who always buys her gifts. She has everything, and I figured she wouldn't miss a coat. On my way home that night, I stuck it into my bag. The next day, Jill sent an e-mail asking for its return. But I didn't want to part with my new gear after all of my friends had gushed over it. A week later, Jill came in wearing a gorgeous new camel coat. Yep, you guessed it...I snagged that one too." —*Carol, 25*

"My coworker left her jacket in the closet. It was so gorgeous that I had to have it...."

Path of Yeast Resistance

"Last summer my boyfriend rented a house on the beach, and even though I was planning to break up with him, I wanted to take full advantage of his place. The problem was, our relationship was so bad that I couldn't even bring myself to have sex with him. Every night he would try, but I kept making up excuses about having chronic yeast infections. When September came and I finally dumped him, he was heartbroken, especially when he found out that I'd been screwing around on him with other guys. One night I was at a party with my friends when he stormed up to me and screamed, 'How did you manage to have sex with other people when you had yeast infections all summer long?' I was completely mortified, but I guess I deserved it for the horrible way I treated him." —*Jamie, 23*

41% OF WOMEN HAVE STOLEN SOMETHING FROM A FRIEND OR COWORKER.

Pity Woman

"I met this girl and went back to her place. We started fooling around, but when I reached for a condom, she put on the brakes. I really wanted to get some, so I lied and told her that ever since my fiancée broke up with me, I hadn't wanted to have sex with anyone…until her. I said that I felt ready to trust again, and her rejection would only open up old wounds. Thankfully, she bought my lame story and gave in." —Jonathan, 26

Breakup Bust

"I had been seeing this guy for a few months when I realized he was a loser. I didn't have the guts to dump him, so I had my friend call him on three-way and tell him my grandma had died. Afterward, my friend thought he had hung up, so we started laughing. I asked her if she thought he believed the story, but our giggles were interrupted when the guy said, 'I did believe it—but not anymore, you bitch!'" —Anita, 31

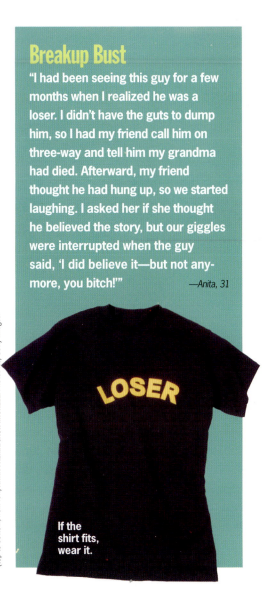

If the shirt fits, wear it.

At the rate this chick's going, she'll break the machine.

PLEASE Take A Number

Two Times a Tart

"My best friend always gets guys, and I admit that I'm jealous. One afternoon I was heading over to meet her at her apartment. She wasn't home yet, so I was there alone with her brother who was in town visiting. One thing led to another, and we ended up having sex. Afterward, he left to meet some of his buddies, but I was not alone for long—my friend's boyfriend arrived 20 minutes later. I was feeling naughty, so I told him how I'd always been attracted to him. He took it from there, and we wound up going at it on the floor. Luckily, my friend didn't show up until we were both dressed and in the clear. She'd be so pissed if she ever found out that I slept with her bro and her beau in the same afternoon!" —Shana, 22

JERK ALERT! ## Re-gift Rogue

"One morning after a random fling, my dad called to make sure I would be on time to my mother's birthday brunch. After the girl left, I noticed she had forgotten her earrings, and it suddenly occurred to me that I didn't have a gift for my mother. So I grabbed the chick's earrings, wrapped them in some newspaper and ribbon, and gave them to Mom. A few days later, the girl called to ask if I had seen her jewelry anywhere. I told her I'd look, then never called her back." —Roger, 23

This innocent bunny became part of a sinister plot.

Phi Delta Psycho

"When I first started college I had a hard time making friends, so I thought that joining a sorority would help. I rushed a whole bunch of houses, but didn't get a single bid. One house had been particularly hurtful to me during the process—ignoring me at functions and giggling behind my back—so I decided to get even. First, I bought a gallon of red paint, sneaked into their backyard, and wrote 'I'm watching you, sluts!' across the wall. A couple of weeks later I bought a scary mask and started standing in front of the first-floor bedroom windows holding a butcher knife. To start, they thought it was a prank, but when they began to receive anonymous threatening letters sent by yours truly, they freaked out and changed all the locks. Late one night when I was driving home from a party, I saw a rabbit carcass by the side of the road. The next morning, the sorority girls woke up to find a dead animal at their front door. A week later, two of the girls dropped out of the sorority and moved off campus." —Jasmine, 21

HAVE YOU EVER CHEATED ON YOUR PARTNER?

55% OF WOMEN SAID YES.

48% OF MEN SAID YES.

Lazy Ploy

"One Monday I came into the office and realized that I had forgotten about a presentation I was supposed to give that morning. I hadn't done a thing to prepare, and I wasn't sure what to do. Then I had an idea: I walked into the meeting, and just as I was about to speak, I pretended to pass out cold. The VPs all rushed to my side and attempted to revive me. When I finally 'came to,' my boss told me to go home, rest up, and give my presentation later that week." —Cynthia, 31

While he was sleepin', she was cheatin'.

Horny Houseguest

"My boyfriend and I accepted an invitation to a friend's beach house one weekend. There was a bunch of other people staying there, including one hottie who kept giving me the eye. Since my guy snores like a bulldozer when he's really zonked, I told him to crash on the couch for the night. Then, half an hour after we all went to bed, I invited the hottie to sneak into my room for some fun. While my man slept on the sofa, I had a wild couple of hours with the cutie. When we were through he went back to his room. No one had any clue what went down." —Sandra, 23

"I want you so much, uh, Lisa...I mean, Carla."

Cruel Come-on

"I was out with my pals when we met this hot chick. She said she liked one of my friends, not me. I was insulted, so I lied and told her that he thought she wasn't cute. When she started to cry, I quickly told her that she was *my* type. After the blow to her ego, my compliments made her feel good, so she gave me a chance. We wound up back at her place." —*Scott, 21*

"I told my buddies to wait outside my apartment window and they'd get the ultimate show...."

Raunch With a View

"I was dating this good-looking woman, but since I've always been unlucky in love, my friends didn't believe me. To prove it, I told the guys to show up at my apartment building at 1 a.m. on a Friday night, sit in their car with the lights off, and at 1:15 they'd get the ultimate show. That night, I asked her if we could do it up against my window. She said she wouldn't mind as long as we closed the blinds. I told her we didn't have to since my windows were tinted, which was a total lie. So my hot woman and I did it up against the glass with my buddies watching down below." —*Jay, 23*

Name Game

"I met this beautiful girl at a club one night, and we ended up back at my house. We had mind-blowing sex, but when I woke up the next morning, I realized I didn't even know her name. I pretended to be sound asleep, hoping she would leave, but she didn't. So I finally rolled over and said, 'Good morning, Nicole.' I knew that wasn't her name and that she'd leave the minute she realized I didn't know what it was. As soon as I said it, her face turned bright red, and she ran out, berating me for being such a jerk." —*Tony, 25*

42% OF MEN HAVE FORGOTTEN THE NAME OF A HOOKUP THE NEXT MORNING.

Pack your bags, pooch. You're outta here!

Dog Gone

"My live-in girlfriend begged me to let her get a dog. I finally agreed on the condition that she would take care of it, because I'm not an animal person. Instead, I was the one who cleaned up after him, walked him, and fed him. I even had to housebreak him! My girlfriend did nothing but play and cuddle with the mutt.

"My girlfriend did nothing but cuddle with the mutt. I got sick of it and hatched a plan."

Finally, I got so sick of dealing with it that I put an ad in the paper and found a nice old lady to take the dog. I dropped it off while my girlfriend was at work and later told her that the dog had run away. She was really upset, but she eventually got over it. After a few months, she suggested that we get another pup, but this time I refused." —*Grant, 28*

HAVE YOU EVER HAD SEX WITH YOUR PARTNER'S FRIEND?

33% OF WOMEN SAID YES.

30% OF MEN SAID YES.

Booty Blackout

"Rebecca, my girlfriend, and I had been living together for a few months, but our hours were really different. One rainy afternoon while she was at work, I invited a female friend of hers over to watch a movie. Pretty soon, we were going at it on the couch. Well, Rebecca ended up getting off early, and she walked in on her friend and me butt naked. She ran out, but wound up slipping on the wet pavement and banging her head. She was unconscious, so I rushed her to the hospital. A couple of hours later she woke up from her concussion. I was afraid she was going to hate me, but as it turns out, she had no memory of what went on." —*Matthew, 29*

Twisted Sister

"When my sister's marriage ended she was heartbroken. Although our entire family was supportive, she especially leaned on me because I was single and also had had lousy luck in relationships. About a year after the divorce, I ran into her ex, and we began to date behind her back. When we announced we were a couple, my sister flipped out. We stopped speaking—and needless to say, we did not request the 'honor of her presence' at our wedding a year later. I know she'll never forgive me for what I did, but I also love my new husband." —*Jeannie, 34*

"Just try and take him from me, and I'll bring on the pain."

Sneaking Suspicion

NAUGHTY, NAUGHTY!

"I had this nagging feeling that my fiancée was not being faithful to me, but I couldn't be totally certain. Finally, I broke down and decided to read her diary. One morning after she headed for the shower, I leapt out of bed, nabbed it out of her hiding place, and started madly flipping through, looking for evidence of her affair. Suddenly, she walked back into the room to grab her towel and caught me. She couldn't believe I would invade her privacy like that, so she threw the ring in my face, kicked me out, and refused to take me back." —*Hugh, 28*

Some things are better left unread.

Erotic Appetizer

"One night my girlfriend and I went out to dinner. There was a long wait for a table, so we sat at the bar to have a drink. When I looked across the room, I saw this girl whom I'd had a fling with a couple of years ago. I remembered how

"I told my girlfriend I had to make a call but instead went to say hello to my former flame."

amazing the sex was, so I told my girlfriend I had to make a phone call, but instead went to say hello to my former flame. After making some small talk for a few minutes, I decided I had nothing to lose and asked her if she wanted to meet me in the bathroom. She took the bait, and we had a quickie in a women's-room stall while my poor girlfriend was sipping her chardonnay out front at the bar." —*Mike, 27*

Wonder what stunt she pulled to put that look of shock on his face

Diaper Duty

"After I caught my fiancé, Brandon, cheating on me with a good friend of mine, I decided that I needed a fresh start, so I moved across the country to California. One Christmas, I was back home grocery shopping with my 18-month-old nephew when I saw Brandon. We made small talk, but the longer I stood there, the more I remembered how much he'd hurt me. So when he asked me who the 'little guy' was, I looked him right in the eye and said, 'He's your son.' Then I told him that I didn't have enough money for diapers and baby food. Somehow, I managed to manipulate him into sending me $200 a month for a child I didn't have. After a year, I was able to buy myself a pair of diamond studs, then I sent him an e-mail saying I no longer needed his money." —Susie, 26

"I was with my nephew when I ran into my ex and decided to have some fun...."

Laid Over

"I was trying to make last-minute plane reservations so I could visit my girlfriend, but there were no available tickets. Finally, one of the customer-service people said she could bump someone off the flight I needed...with one catch: She wanted to see me during my two-hour layover in a connecting city. Apparently, she was intrigued by my deep voice. I agreed to meet her and go for a drink at the airport cocktail lounge. She was gorgeous, so I missed my flight to visit my girlfriend and spent my vacation with the mysterious airline woman." —Mike, 35

Tequila Sunrise

"Back in college I had a really rocky relationship with my girlfriend. One spring break a whole group of us took a trip down to Mexico. On our third night there my girlfriend was bothering me, so I disappeared into a club and found a superhot girl to hang out with. After more than a few margaritas, we ended up sneaking out and getting a hotel room together. I didn't wake up until six the next morning. My buddies knew I was probably with another woman, but my girlfriend was worried. When I finally returned, I told them that I had been arrested for public drunkenness by the Mexican police and had to spend the night in jail. My girlfriend didn't nag me at all for the rest of the trip." —Chris, 27

"Here's to a steamy night in Mexico."

Oh, if only this chair could talk.

3

SOMEBODY SPANK HIM!

Reclining-Chair Romp

"One night my fiancée, Joanne, and I went on a double date with her hot friend Cecie and her husband, Ron. We went to dinner, then headed to their place to hang out. Joanne was passed out on the couch, but the three of us stayed up. When Ron ran out to grab something from the store, his wife and I started going at it on her husband's reclining chair. Meanwhile, Joanne was passed out on the couch next to us! By the time Cecie's hubby got back, we were hanging out as if nothing had happened." —Craig, 28

Lax Experience

"I'd been out of work for months and was having trouble finding a job. One of my friends, Molly, got laid off around the same time, so we were both job hunting. One day I heard about this amazing opportunity. When I told Molly, she got really quiet and then informed me that she was interviewing for that spot. I tried to mask my jealousy and invited her over for dinner the night before her interview. I made her chicken Parmesan, but added a special ingredient to hers: laxatives. The next morning, she had such bad diarrhea that she had to cancel the interview." —Carla, 27

"HIS PSYCHO EX WOULDN'T GO AWAY"

We've all been crazy about a special guy, but these chicks are just plain *crazy*. Read on to find out what happens to schizos who don't understand the meaning of O-V-E-R.

"Don't look now, but the bitch is back."

Pooch Ploy

"My boyfriend's ex, Cassandra, was always a little on the nutty side, which is part of the reason why he dumped her in the first place. Once she sent a desperate e-mail to him on Valentine's Day, begging him to go to Las Vegas with her and get married, despite the fact that he was already involved in a serious relationship with me. I thought that was pretty crazy, but then a week or two later, she showed up with a brand-new puppy at the dog park we go to every Sunday. That might not seem so strange, except the park we go to is a 45-minute car ride from where she lives, and Cassandra has always hated dogs with a passion. It was so obvious that she had bought a dog just so she could ruin our Sunday-afternoon ritual." —*Annie, 24*

Betty Crackpot

"Although they had split up more than a year earlier, my boyfriend's ex, Lisa, wouldn't leave him alone. She constantly called Tyler, wanting details about our sex life and asking if the sex with me was as good as it had been with her. She also kept telling him that he needed someone who would make a good wife, and to emphasize her point, she started sending him pies and casseroles at least once a week. Even though the food looked incredible, we were both afraid she was going to give us salmonella poisoning or something, so we always threw it out right away." —*Stephanie, 32*

Check out this season's hottest look: stalker chic.

Road Rage

"The more my beau ignored his ex, the crazier she became. Things really got out of control when we ran into her at a restaurant. She followed us out to his car and threw herself onto the hood. My boyfriend started the car anyway and let it roll forward slightly, so she jumped down and began banging on his window. My boyfriend hit the gas, and we took off with the ex chasing us on foot down the street. Later that night back at his house, we heard her yelling obscenities outside. We looked out the window to find her standing on his front lawn, holding a candle." —*Charlotte, 25*

"When my guy's ex found out we were getting married, she went nuts!"

Flower Derangement

"When Craig's ex found out that we were getting married, she went nuts! She started calling our apartment at all hours. Craig told Darcy to go away, but she wasn't getting the message. A month before the wedding, Craig came home to find a giant cardboard heart on the floor with the words 'Darcy and Craig 4Ever' spelled out in rose petals on it. There was a big red box in the center of the 'arrangement.' When he opened it, a helium balloon that said 'I Love You' floated to the ceiling." —*Pauline, 25*

FREAK ALERT!

Undercover Kook

"My boyfriend Jason's ex, Tiffany, was obsessed with him to the point that she would use her old key to get into his place and sleep in his bed when he was out. My boyfriend had the locks changed, but that didn't keep her from breaking in. Once we came home and found that Tiffany had left naked pictures of herself all over the apartment. She'd also thrown out my toiletries and slashed a photo of us. Then, when we went into his bedroom, we found her hiding under the comforter. She refused to leave, so we spent the night in a hotel." —*Angela, 27*

HOW TO...

KEEP YOUR COOL

Remember this when his former flame goes wacko:

Her behavior is not a reason to get angry at him.

Sure the late-night hang ups may be making you miserable, but it's not exactly a picnic for your partner either. Let him know that she is complicating your relationship, but don't blame him.

It's really not your place to deal with it.

As much as you'd like to lash out, just back off. Walk away if she approaches you, and stay out of her spats with your beau. If she becomes threatening, your guy should tell the police.

If you've ever been dumped, you understand how crushing it can be.

And since you don't know for sure whether your guy gave her false hope, it's only fair to give her time to get over him.

SOURCES: SHERRY AMATENSTEIN, AUTHOR OF *LOVE LESSONS FROM BAD BREAKUPS*; DR. PAUL W. COLEMAN, AUTHOR OF *THE COMPLETE IDIOT'S GUIDE TO INTIMACY*

Girl, you need to learn how to let go.

Psycho Beach Party

"After dating for six months Tim and I took a romantic trip to the beach. On the second day, we were sunbathing when we saw someone with binoculars staring at us. We weren't too concerned about it until later that night: We were chilling in our cabana when we heard a noise outside our window. We called hotel security, and they caught Tim's ex trying to peek through the keyhole in our door. She had cut her hair short so we wouldn't recognize her trailing us."
—Lanie, 22

WHY SHE CAN'T MOVE ON

Assuming his ex isn't insane, a couple of things could be going on: First off, she may be so narcissistic that she feels she "owns" this man and can have him back. Or, she could be disillusioned enough to believe that if he knew how much she loved him, he'd want to reconcile.

SOURCE: IRENE MATIATOS, PHD, PSYCHOLOGIST IN ORANGE COUNTY, NEW YORK

"We were having a great time until his ex got up on stage, crying hysterically."

Loony Tune

"One night I went with some friends, including my new beau, Brandon, to a karaoke bar. We were having a great time when a woman got up on stage, crying hysterically. It was Brandon's ex! With mascara streaming down her face she sang a freakishly psychotic rendition of 'I Will Always Love You.' Horrified, we quickly stood up to leave, when his ex, with arms outstretched, started yelling to Brandon, begging him to come back to her."
—Lucy, 23

"Next up, straight from the asylum..."

OUCH!
BOOTY SESSIONS GONE VERY, VERY WRONG

When it's good, sex can be a bed-bouncing, high-octane experience. But as these cautionary tales show, sometimes erotic aerobics can go awry…and hurt like hell.

ANNA PALMA

We've heard of turning up the heat, but this is ridiculous.

5

Carnal Crash Course

"When my girlfriend Lisa's parents went out of town one weekend, they asked if we could dog-sit for them. Lisa and I were totally psyched about it because we were looking forward to christening every room in the house. On our first night there we went right to the living room. Lisa and I were going at it on the couch when I decided to lift her onto the glass coffee table. I was convinced that it was sturdy enough to take our weight. Well, I was wrong, because all of a sudden we heard a crack, followed by a crash, as we fell right through the table. I quickly pulled Lisa out of the glass heap, but there were shards imbedded in her butt. We wrapped her bloody behind in a towel and rushed to the emergency room. The doctors stitched up the deep cuts and sent us home, but it was a good two weeks before she was able to sit down without feeling any pain. She still has the battle scars to this day." —Chris, 31

Hot Dish!

"For our first anniversary, I decided to whip up my man's favorite meal for him, and I thought it would be hot to do all the cooking in the nude. While my man sat at the kitchen table, I strutted around in nothing but my high heels. After awhile, I guess he couldn't stand the anticipation anymore because he came up from behind me, began kissing my neck, and we started going at it. Unfortunately, though, between the high heels and all the action, I wound up losing my balance and falling back against the hot oven. I yelped in pain and crumpled to the floor. Luckily, I only ended up with a minor burn on my back, but that's the last time I cook in the nude!" —Teri, 23

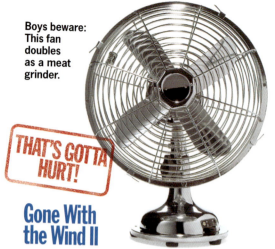

Boys beware: This fan doubles as a meat grinder.

THAT'S GOTTA HURT!

Gone With the Wind II

"My girlfriend's apartment gets really hot at night. Every time I'm there and we have sweaty sex, I go over to her rickety old fan afterward and stand in front of it to cool off. One evening after we finished doing it, I slipped out of bed and stood near the fan. Since the lights were out, I couldn't see that she'd taken off the front guard, and I inched closer to get cool air between my legs. Suddenly, it felt like dozens of rubber bands were snapping at my penis. I screamed and backed away. Fortunately, the plastic blade was moving so slowly, I only got red marks, but the burning sensation was still really bad in the morning." —*Alex, 21*

Trip Tease

"My boyfriend Jack spent the summer studying for his law boards. The day after the test, I planned an extra-special seduction: a striptease he'd never forget. The moment he stepped into his bedroom, he got a huge grin on his face. I told him to make himself comfortable in bed while I slowly and seductively peeled off my clothing. Everything was going as planned until I got my jeans down around my ankles. That's when I lost my balance, fell, and hit my mouth on the bedpost. My guy leaped

"My seduction was going as planned until I fell and cracked my tooth!"

up and helped me into the bathroom to wash the blood off my face. When I looked in the mirror, I saw that my front tooth was cracked in half! We ended up rushing to my dentist's office where, luckily, I was able to get a crown attached." —*Isabel, 28*

EXCUSES, EXCUSES
These explanations might help reduce X-rated-accident embarrassment.

THE INJURY	THE EXPLANATION
Fractured penis	"He hurt it playing dodge ball."
Below-the-belt food allergy	"Geez, I always spill when I eat dinner naked!"
Concussion from headboard banging	"I'm on an aggressive intramural soccer team."
Pulled groin muscle	"Damn that power yoga!"

"Uh-oh, we may have to cut it off. Just kidding, buddy."

Out With a Bang

"On my boyfriend's birthday last year, his friends threw a huge party for him, and we flirted like crazy all night. When we got home later we were horny beyond belief, so things got pretty wild. At one point, we were doing the deed doggie-style, and my head kept banging against the headboard. I don't know if I was just in the moment or what, but I barely felt it. The next day I woke up with a killer headache, so I took some aspirin and went to work. I felt really lightheaded, though, and the pain wasn't going away. Midmorning, I was at the copier when I suddenly passed out. My coworkers rushed over, and one of them called an ambulance. I was taken to the hospital immediately. Apparently, all that head banging the night before had given me a pretty serious concussion." —Tanya, 23

Bumps in the Night

"My girlfriend Joanna and I thought it would be fun to use food during sex. We put an old sheet on the bed and pulled out a plethora of food products. We took turns covering each other with whipped cream, strawberries, and chocolate syrup, and then licking it off, but we paid for it later. After our erotic adventure, we were so exhausted that we fell asleep. In the middle of the night Joanna woke up complaining that she felt as though she had rolled around in poison ivy. When I turned on the light, I saw that she had a rash and tiny bumps all over her body. We went straight to the ER, where a doctor told Joanna she was having an allergic reaction. As embarrassing as it was, we came clean. The doc said the combination of foods and saliva had irritated her skin." —Rick, 33

"We took turns covering each other with whipped cream and chocolate syrup, but we paid for it later."

Sexy Smackdown

"T.J. and I had been dating for just over a month, and I was totally hot for him. So one night after a really romantic dinner, I told him I had to have him. As soon as we got to his place, the clothes came off at lightning speed. After pulling his pants down to his ankles, I popped back up to kiss him, but my head smacked him right in the nose. He yelled out in pain as blood spurted everywhere. The bleeding wouldn't stop, so we had to get him to the hospital. My head butt had broken his nose." —Vanessa, 23

Bad to the Bone

"After months of flirting, this hot coworker of mine finally asked me out. On our first date things were going so well that we ended up sleeping together. That night, I was dying of thirst, but Dennis was sleeping, and I needed to crawl past him to get out. I stood up on the bed and tiptoed around his body. Suddenly he turned over, and I fell, my palm smacking down hard onto his package. He started screaming in pain, and I ran to get ice. He wouldn't talk to me for days. We worked things out, though… after he stopped limping."

—Danielle, 24

"I stood up and tiptoed around him….The next thing I knew, he was screaming in pain."

Showstopper

"My fiancé, Bill, was crazy about watching girls belly dance, so I secretly took lessons and planned to surprise him on his birthday. After we ate a home-cooked meal, I changed into my costume and started the show. Unfortunately, the wine went straight to my head, and I got dizzy, slammed into the wall, and threw out my back. I was in so much pain that I couldn't even move. Bill carried me into the bedroom, helped me undress, brought me aspirin, and put me to bed. He was also stuck washing all the dirty dishes. It was definitely not the birthday celebration he had hoped for."

—Sabrina, 30

Twisted Tryst

"A couple of months ago, while my girlfriend and I were having sex, she decided to see just how flexible she was by bending her legs as far back as she could. I was totally into it, so I started leaning on her legs to see how much more she could take. Well, that was a bad idea. All of a sudden she felt a pop in her knee and screamed at the top of her lungs. When I looked at her leg, it was clear that something wasn't right, so we went to the hospital. As it turned out, she'd dislocated her knee." —David, 30

In a Lather

"I was so excited about this date I had that I decided to engage in some self-pleasure in the shower using a shampoo bottle. Big mistake. My member got stuck! I had to cancel my date, telling her an emergency had come up. Then I had to go to the hospital to have the bottle removed. You should have heard me try to explain to the nurse why my unit was stuck in a shampoo bottle." —Tim, 22

This little guy's seen things a duck should never see.

All Washed Up

"Last summer my boyfriend and I planned a long romantic weekend at a bed-and-breakfast in Cape Cod. When we arrived at the place, I discovered that there was a tiny laundry room in the basement. I'd always been curious about sex on a washing machine, so when nobody was around, I led him downstairs. After taking off all of our clothes, I turned on the machine and hopped on top. My man stood in front of

"The motion of the machine felt great beneath me until all of a sudden it made a loud booming noise!"

me and we started going at it like crazy. The motion of the machine felt great beneath me, until, all of a sudden, it made a loud booming noise. I was so startled that I screamed and jumped onto my guy, who fell over and slammed into a table. His head split open, and there was blood everywhere! I put my clothes on as fast as I could, then grabbed my cell and dialed 911. He ended up getting 23 stitches! And the B&B's owner kicked us out for breaking his machine." —*Taryn, 27*

74% OF READERS HAVE HURT THEMSELVES OR THEIR PARTNERS WHILE GETTING IT ON.

"It was hot, so I took off my clothes. Too bad I'd forgotten that my front door was open...."

'MY ACCIDENTAL FLASHER MOMENT"

From T to A and much, much more, these men and women gave an unsuspecting audience quite an eyeful.

6

Mini Melodrama

"Last summer I met my girlfriends in Las Vegas for a wild weekend. On our first night, we planned to go to this three-story club. I'd bought a super-tight miniskirt that day and I decided to go sans undies. I mean, after all, we were in Vegas! Later that night I was talking to a hunky guy when I spilled my drink on my shoe. When I looked down to see if it had left a mark, I got quite a surprise: The floor under the bar was made of colored panes of glass, and I happened to be standing on one of the clear panes. I could see through it to the dance floor below, where there were three guys pointing up at me. After that humiliating experience, I'll never go commando again!" —Lily, 24

Special Delivery

"It was summertime, my AC had shut down, and I was way too broke to buy a new one. So one night when the temperature got up to the mid-90's, I took off all of my clothes and just sat in front of the fan in my underwear. In the meantime, I ordered myself a pizza, but I figured I'd throw on a tee shirt and shorts when I heard the door-bell ring. Well, I guess in my overheated stupor I'd left the front door ajar because, out of nowhere, I heard 'Um, excuse me, miss?' I turned to find a very red-faced delivery guy standing there with one hand over his eyes and my pizza in the other. Mortified, I handed the man a $20 and told him to keep the change." —Tanya, 23

Some poor pooches take the rap for everything.

Wet Puppies

"I wore one of those water bras and a low-cut shirt to introduce myself to my sexy new neighbor. As we were talking, I noticed his adorable Chihuahua and scooped him up in my arms. Right at that moment, a car alarm started blaring, and

"The dog dug its nails into my shirt and popped my water bra!"

the jumpy little dog freaked out. He dug his supersharp nails into my shirt and popped my bra. Before I knew it, my top was completely soaked, and you could see my nipples. Luckily, my neighbor thought his puppy had peed on me, so I got sympathy out of the deal." —LaTosha, 25

41% OF WOMEN HAVE ACCIDENTALLY SHOWED THEIR BUTTS IN PUBLIC.

Shorts Changed

"For Memorial Day my company held a corny cookout for the employees, so I showed up at the lake and played horseshoes with some of the head honchos. After I put in my time, I decided to sneak out, but I had to pee first. The bathrooms were all the way on the other side of the lake, so I decided to duck behind some bushes. Just as I dropped my shorts, I looked up and saw half of my department waving at me from a boat on the water. Back at the office, everyone called me Squatting Sue." —Susan, 31

LOL!

Not really office attire

Pantie Raid

"Not only do my boyfriend and I work for the same company, but I'm his supervisor. One morning, he walked past my office and asked me what day it was. I stood up and said, 'Dress-up day, baby,' and then lifted up my skirt for him to see my new lace panties. Not only did *he* get a show, but so did our boss—who was walking by just as I did my little peekaboo act. I'd have gotten canned if I'd revealed our relationship, so instead, I got written up for violating the company's sexual-harassment policy." —Juliet, 21

Note to self:
Remember
to burn the
tape next time.

News Flash

"For a broadcast journalism class, I had to videotape myself conducting an interview with a friend. I picked my boyfriend, and after we wrapped up my assignment, we decided to pop in a new tape and make a, *ahem*, private movie. In class the next day my professor was showing all the videos. But when he cued up the 'interview' I did, my naked breasts filled the screen. I'd mixed up the tapes! I turned bright red, grabbed the tape out of the VCR, and ran!"   —Sheila, 21

Electrifying Moment

"As I rushed from my office for a job interview, I had to make a couple of pit stops along the way. That involved me taking my coat off quite a few times. I knew my hair was getting full of static electricity, but I didn't realize the extent of the problem. At the interview, the guy I met with helped me out of my coat and said, "Well, you've got the job." I didn't understand the joke at first, but then he pointed me to a mirror. Somehow, with all my frantic movement and my coat shifting, I had created so much static electricity that my dress was bunched up over my hips. Of course I wasn't wearing underwear with my nylons, so my interviewer got a look at my nearly bare ass! I blushed through the rest of the interview, and I was so mortified by the entire experience that when he called to offer me the job, I couldn't accept it."   —Faith, 26

6

From now on, she's a pants-only girl.

> "I knew my hair was getting full of static electricity, but I didn't realize the extent of the problem."

These boxers gave one old lady the thrill of her life.

Oldie But a Woody

"One warm Sunday morning I woke up early and walked out of my house in my boxers to grab the paper. As I bent over to pick it up, I heard my neighbor, a 73-year-old single woman, say, 'That's quite good for a man your age!' I looked down and realized that my prominent morning wood was popping out of the slit in my boxers. She was staring at it like she hadn't seen a penis in years, which I'm fairly certain she hadn't! Every time I see her now she gives me this disturbing pervy smile and reminds me about the incident. She even told my grandmother about it."
—Ryan, 30

Porno Painting

"My ex-girlfriend is a painter, and on a few occasions she asked me to pose nude for her. I agreed as long as she promised not to show her work outside of the classroom. Well, a couple of years after we broke up, I went on a date with another artist who suggested we check out a gallery exhibit downtown. It turned out to be my ex-girlfriend's show. I thought it was a weird coincidence, but didn't see any need for alarm, that is, until we rounded a corner and

"I let my ex paint a nude portrait of me....Little did I know where it would turn up!"

spotted a painting of yours truly, completely naked, covering an entire wall. To make matters worse, she had used some creative license (and post-breakup bitterness) and had shrunk my member to munchkin proportions. My date found it funny and asked, 'Was this drawn to scale?' I never forgave my ex."
—Kevin, 28

CELEBS SHOW THEIR STUFF

Apparently, these stars want us to pay attention to their private lives *and* their privates.

Put it away, PARIS— we've seen it all before.

WHOOPSIE!

WHOOPSIE!

Just when you thought MARIAH'S skirts couldn't get any shorter...

WHOOPSIE!

TARA REID vows to be famous for *something*, damn it.

Church Member

"One Sunday morning I was supposed to give a reading at church, but I overslept. When I finally woke up, I threw on my clothes and left. I made it there in time, and everything went smoothly…or so I thought. As I stepped down from the podium, everyone's jaws dropped. I realized that my penis had flopped out of my pants in front of the entire congregation! In my haste to get ready, I'd decided to go commando and hadn't zipped my fly. For the rest of the service, I slouched in the pew." —Russ, 19

Who knew one pen could create so many problems?

Let Her Rip

"I work at an advertising firm, and recently they hired this amazingly hot guy. One afternoon I noticed him checking out my butt, so I purposely dropped my pen and then bent down slowly to pick it up. Just as I grabbed it, my pants split down the seam, exposing my hot pink panties. It took me a full minute to stand up and face him. Thankfully, when I finally turned around, the cutie was such a gentleman that he took off his dress shirt and gave it to me to tie around my waist." —Michelle, 29

We wouldn't mind if this stud flashed us accidentally.

Ski and Be Seen

OOPS!

"My friends and I were camping at Lake Tahoe, and we saw a group of hot girls, so we pitched our tent right next to theirs and struck up a conversation. They'd rented a boat and invited us to go water-skiing with them. I hadn't skied much, but I wasn't about to let a bunch of chicks show me up. So in an attempt to impress them, I told the driver to haul ass. She started going so fast that as the boat pulled me out of the water, my trunks fell to my ankles. All of a sudden I was skiing naked with my junk flying in the wind! I tried to pull up my suit, but I lost my balance and fell flat on my face. My bathing suit was so far behind me that I had to jump back in the boat and sit there nude while we went to fish it out of the lake." —Adam, 27

"I crawled down my fire escape to the street, where I gave the firemen quite a show."

Smokey the Bare

"One night I was sound asleep when the fire alarm went off. Before I could even open my door, I noticed a little bit of smoke coming in underneath it, so I grabbed my photo album and crawled down the fire escape to the street below. I was surprised to find that no one else had evacuated the building yet, so I started screaming 'Fire! Fire!' Everyone in the front of the building came to their windows and yelled at me to keep it down. Apparently, there was no fire—my neighbor had just burned something in his oven, which was where the smoke had been coming from. Then, as if that weren't humiliation enough, I looked down and realized I was wearing nothing but my underwear." —Linda, 23

This was one false alarm the fire department didn't mind.

15%
OF WOMEN HAVE BEEN SEEN NAKED BY A MEMBER OF THEIR BOYFRIEND'S FAMILY.

Mother Superior

"My girlfriend Shannon invited me to her parents' house for dinner one Saturday. Shannon was out picking up dessert, so her supersexy mom offered me a seat on the couch across from her. But when I sat down on the sofa, she got a horrified expression on her face. I glanced down and noticed that my fly was open and my little guy was standing at attention. I quickly stuffed it back in, and we both pretended nothing had happened. But after I left, her mom filled my girlfriend in. Shannon called me later, told me I was a perv, and then dumped me." —Joe, 21

Such a Boob

"My friends and I went to a disco-theme party at a huge club. We all dressed in low-cut, tight, shiny outfits. I even won a prize for my costume, and when I went onstage to receive my award, the cute guy next to me started pulling some wild John Travolta moves. He lifted me up and was bouncing and jostling me so much that one of my boobs popped right out of the skimpy top I had on. Of course, my friends saw my show and still harass me about it." —Emma, 22

"In the middle of my striptease I threw open the curtains and got the surprise of my life."

Head Over Heels

Sexy, but dangerous

"I wanted to look hot for my date with Steve, so I splurged on a short, flirty skirt and a pair of sexy heels. When I got to the restaurant, I really had to pee. I was early, so I made a beeline for the bathroom. Unfortunately, there was a line, and I leaked a little, so I had to throw my undies out. As I was walking back out to the bar area, I saw Steve waiting and waved. Then, suddenly, my heel got caught in a groove in the wooden floor, and I went flying onto my face, completely exposing my bare ass."

—Amanda, 20

Show 'n' Motel

BAD GIRL

"My boyfriend and I were chilling out in our motel room in Florida when I decided to do a little striptease for him. I had the radio blasting, and I was totally getting my groove on. The windows in our room faced the parking lot, so I thought it would be funny if I shimmied over to the glass and flashed whomever might be outside. It was the afternoon, and though the walkway was right outside our window, I figured most of the kids would be at the beach. Well, when I threw open the curtains, I got the surprise of my life: A father and his two young sons happened to be walking by at that moment. I quickly shut the curtains, but it was too late.... They'd seen me in the buff. I still wonder if the little ones were scarred for life."

—Diane, 24

This guy can sleep over at our office anytime.

Dual-purpose tissues: to stuff a bra and wipe away the tears of humiliation

Busting Loose

"Last year on my birthday my friends were taking me out to a club, and I wanted to look special. I don't have much cleavage, so, to compensate, I bought a low-cut shirt and filled my bra with tissues. I was actually pretty impressed with the effect and knew I would be turning some heads. Did I ever! After hours of dancing and drinking, I started getting more than my fair share of stares. Finally, one of my friends took me aside and pointed out that not only were tissues falling out of my shirt, but both of my little buddies were in plain view—and standing at attention!" —Virginia, 24

Birthday Suit

"One night last year, I stayed really late at the office to work on a project that was due the next day. No one was around, so I took off my suit to get more comfortable. At three in the morning I realized I needed some sleep, but I still had work to do. I called my girlfriend and asked her to wake me at 5:30. Well, she overslept, and I woke up the next morning to find the president of the company standing over me. He actually praised me for all my hard work…right after he told me to put my clothes back on." —Andrew, 31

Full-Frontal Flash

"I was going to the beach for the weekend and needed a last-minute Brazilian wax. My regular waxer couldn't take me, so I had no choice but to run into one of those quickie nail salons. They brought me into a back room, and the woman asked me to take off my underwear and lie on a table. She then said she'd be right back. Well, she didn't shut the door completely, because, while I was lying there butt naked, it swung open, exposing me to the entire salon. I screamed, drawing even more attention to myself, then ran over to shut it. I was so humiliated that I got the heck out of there ASAP." —Gretchen, 31

"I stayed late at the office and took off my suit to get more comfortable...."

Meat-and-Potatoes Guy

"I was out to dinner with my girlfriend at this really upscale steakhouse. During the meal I got up to go to the bathroom and forgot to zip my pants afterward. When I sat back down at the table, my girl started rubbing her toes up my leg. I became so aroused that my member shot right out of my pants. Apparently, our snarky waiter noticed, because while opening our bottle of wine, he said, 'It looks like you already popped your cork, buddy.' I was beet red while I finished my meal, but the waiter thought it was really funny and kept cracking jokes at my expense for the rest of the evening." —Mick, 30

Too bad he didn't pop his cork in the privacy of his own home

2001

Don't wear this to meet the parents.

UH-OH

Flash Pants

"I had been dating Jason for a couple of months when he decided to bring me home to meet his mother. Unfortunately, he hadn't told me about the plan ahead of time, so I wasn't dressed appropriately. I thought we were going to the park, and I was sporting track pants and a grungy

"This guy I was dating brought me to his mom's house. Unfortunately, I wasn't dressed appropriately...."

tee shirt. I begged Jason to let me go home and change, but he assured me that I looked fine. As we walked up the front steps, though, my pants snagged on the railing and ripped from crotch to hip, exposing my bright blue thong. Luckily, though, Jason's mom was really sweet about it and gave me something else to put on, but it was still a pretty embarrassing first impression." —April, 20

"I'VE SEEN IT ALL—FROM BOLD FEMALES BARING THEIR BREASTS TO CLUELESS GUYS USING LAME PICKUP LINES."

CONFESSIONS OF
A Bartender

A loose-lipped mixologist spills about the wild women who've hit on him, the outrageous antics of misbehaving patrons, and more….

■ Think of the craziest thing you've done after a night of bar hopping. Maybe you and your friends competed for who could leave with the most phone numbers. Or perhaps you decided to do a groovy little dance atop your bar stool. If so, don't worry; you're not alone.

Having been in the bar/club business for 11 years, I've seen it all—from bold females baring their breasts to clueless guys using lame pickup lines. Sure, most bar-goers are just looking to kick back and have a good time. But before you embark on your next pub crawl, I've got some eye-opening insights for you. Bartenders are watching, and we're always there to hear your story. Now I want to tell you mine.

At Your Service

Bartending is full of obvious perks. Who could resist a fun, fast-paced job and the opportunity to make loads of cash? On a good night, I can pull in $700. But over the years, I've gained something else—the ability to tap into what makes people, especially women, tick. And that's a benefit that can't be measured in dollars.

Like many guys, my listening skills were lousy before I stepped behind a bar. But to be truly successful, I needed to know more than just how to make a mean martini. I had to play psychologist. It's a give-and-take that makes sense—I pour you a glass, you pour out your sorrows.

Along the way I've had to learn how to listen…and it's paid off big time. As the booze flows, girls have opened up to me about everything from their cheating boyfriends to their slave-driving bosses to their sex lives. I lend an ear, try to allay their fears, and more often than not, eventually make a connection. Some chicks will subtly compliment my eyes, while others will slip me their digits along with a tip. I know what you're wondering. Have I ever taken them home? Uh, you bet I have!

"A STATUESQUE BLOND CAME ON TO ME AND I COULDN'T RESIST INVITING HER TO MY PLACE. SHE QUICKLY WORE OUT HER WELCOME, THOUGH."

In an average evening, I'll flirt with dozens of women, but there's usually one in particular who'll catch my eye. I'll feed her extra-strong drinks—for free, of course—until we can hook up when my shift is over at 4 a.m. Most of the time, it's for one night only, and we'll part amicably in the morning. But every once in a while, I wind up with a real nutcase on my hands.

How'd you like one of these babies thrown in your face?

Case in point: One time, a statuesque blond came on to me, and I couldn't resist inviting her back to my place. She quickly wore out her welcome, though. At the bar, I thought she was handling her liquor all right, but at my place I could see she was drunk. Even though she was all over me, I didn't want to take advantage of her, so I made her some coffee instead. She was really pissed that I wouldn't fool around with her and screamed, "Do you know how many men would give their left ball to sleep with me?"

Then she headed to my shelves and started pummeling me with books and CDs! I grabbed a hold of her before she totally wrecked my apartment and led her out. But she continued banging on my door until I called the cops to haul her away! Apparently, some girls just refuse to take no for an answer.

Out-of-Control Customers

I've seen plenty of wacky behavior in the bar too. Once, during one of my shifts, the coat-check guy came running down the stairs shouting, "They're fighting! They're fighting in the coat-check room right now!" Three big, burly bouncers rushed over only to find a guy and a girl half naked and going at it like bunnies. The coat-check guy had an accent, and what we thought was "fighting" was actually "f#!@ing."

Some customers refuse to keep their clothes on. A woman once climbed onto the bar, dropped her pants, and jiggled her ass for the crowd. She almost caused a riot, but she was having so much fun, we let her finish.

"I don't know what's prettier: the drink or the guy pouring it."

Not all antics involve sex and nudity, though. There are customers—usually petite girls—who don't seem to know their limit. One minute, they're the life of the party; the next, they're slumped over the bar.

Guys could use a primer on handling their liquor too. Recently, a frat boy was celebrating his 21st birthday. I made sure he wouldn't be driving before I let him get tanked. After his fifth shot (in half an hour), his face turned beet red, and he let out a groan the likes of which I'd never heard a human emit. He started to head to the bathroom, but his stomach couldn't wait, and he wound up barfing all over a poor girl's designer handbag. His friends thought it was hilarious, but the woman was PO'd.

When my customers aren't ruining someone else's night, they're creating problems for themselves. If you plan on getting a little buzzed, ladies, wear shoes you can walk in.

One night, I saw a girl teetering around in five-inch heeled sandals, and I knew she was headed for a spill. At one point, she attempted to get up, but her heel was hooked on the stool. She fell headfirst and was knocked out cold. The worst part? Her friends were so busy

THE CHEESIEST PICKUP LINES EVER

"You must be tired, because you've been running through my mind all day."

"Is your dad a butcher? Because you're one fine piece of meat."

"I'm sorry, did you say something? I'm mesmerized by your beauty."

"Can I see the tag on your shirt? Just what I thought: Made in heaven."

These heels could cost you in more ways than one.

"MEN LIKE TO THINK THEY'R THEY'RE LOOKING TO HAVE

partying, they let her lie there for a few minutes before they finally picked her up. Unfortunately, it was a busy night, and I was too swamped behind the bar to help her out.

Gender Blender

Craziness aside, I can honestly say that what goes on inside the bar is a microcosm of male-female relationships. Men like to think they're in charge, but women call most of the shots—and they're looking to have just as much no-strings-attached fun. And even though men size up the opposite sex like a lecherous pack of wolves, girls can be just as ravenous.

After a few drinks, some women will suck face with anything that moves—including

other girls. Men love to watch, but they're less enthusiastic when she pulls the same stunt with different guys. I've seen girls make out with one dude, then, when he leaves for a minute, find someone else. By the time the first guy comes back, she's already sucking face with someone else.

Despite all the outrageous behavior, I have seen lots of legitimate hookups and relationships develop. If you'd like to meet someone of substance—yes, believe it or not, good guys do frequent the bar scene—my advice is to keep serious talk to an absolute minimum. Sure, you want to know what a guy does for a living, but don't grill him about where he lives, what his apartment is like, and what kind of car he drives. It's so tacky, not to mention incredibly shallow. Instead, you're better off sticking to light topics, and, when he's ready, he'll open up to you on his own.

It also helps to be patient. If a guy you've had your eye on finally comes over to you and your crew, but ends up talking with your

MEN BEHAVING VERY BADLY

Female bartenders reveal the slimy male antics they've observed on the job.

"Men on business trips usually tip well, but recently, this guy drank for four hours and left a five-dollar tip. I sarcastically said I would put it toward my college fund, and he stuffed some twenties in his pants and slurred, 'Nothing in life is free. Come and get it!' I didn't take him up on the offer." —Roni, 22

"This guy came in with his date, who seemed to really like him—even though he kept staring at my chest. She got pretty tipsy, so I told him to call a car service for her. He left, then returned alone. An hour later I went to the ATM and found the chick wandering around. The creep had left her outside!" —Nicole, 3

This lucky lady looks shaken and stirred.

friends, he most likely isn't ignoring you. Often, a man will make small talk with a girl's pals as a decoy. Then, when his nerves have settled, he'll turn his attention to you. Just give it time to see how things play out.

Another tip: Whatever you do, don't let a man buy you drinks all night long when you have absolutely no interest in him. You will just lead him on, which is unfair and kind of mean. I've witnessed guys getting belligerent when a greedy girl has taken them for a ride. It's easier just to buy your own drinks.

I've picked up a few pointers as well over the years. Dealing with all sorts of different personality types has taught me how to be comfortable in practically any situation—whether I'm trying to meet a woman outside of work or I just want to get to know someone better at a party. Plus, my job lets me look at cute babes all night, hear good music, and have fun. What in the world could be better than that? If it weren't for bartending, I never would have had those opportunities. Unless, of course, I was a rock star! ∎

"One time, this guy at my bar told a girl, 'Your behind is like a ripe peach. Can I have a bite?' She said, 'No, but you can have a taste of this' and splashed a full drink on him. I was so impressed with the chick's guts that I hooked her up with free cocktails for the rest of the night." —Laura, 24

"I work at a hotel bar, and one night an attractive woman came in with her teenage son. This loser at the end of the bar kept making crude comments to her, right in front of her son. After a few remarks about her breasts, he yelled for her to lose the kid and come back to his place. At that point, we kicked him out." —Alicia, 24

"When I heard the keys in the door, I posed seductively on the couch. But it wasn't my boyfriend who walked in!"

'OOPS! I MADE A MOVE ON THE WRONG GUY!"

You may think it's close to impossible to accidentally seduce your beau's brother or spank the butt of a virtual stranger. But somehow these readers made it happen.

8

Twin Cheeks

"Even though I'd only been on a few dates with Chris, he was so sexy that I ended up sleeping with him pretty quickly. One Saturday before I went out with some girlfriends, I left a message on Chris's cell phone, telling him to meet us at the bar. Finally just as I was leaving, he walked in. I told him to take me home right away and make love to me. We couldn't keep our hands off each other as we stumbled back to my place. The sex was even better than I'd remembered. The next morning, when I went to wake him, I noticed a tattoo of a spider on his butt that I had never seen before. I asked him about it and he said he got it years ago. After much confusion, we figured out the mix-up: I had just had sex with Chris's twin brother, whom I never even knew existed!" —Carrie, 23

Welcome Moan

"My boyfriend Grant had been having a rough week, so, after work on Friday, I decided to help him relax by planning a sexy surprise. Grant's roommate was going away to visit his family for the weekend, so we'd be alone. I spent an hour setting the mood with candles, red scarves, and fresh sheets. I even slipped on a new see-through black teddy. When I heard keys in the door, I quickly turned off all the lights, posed seductively on the couch, and began moaning lustfully, 'I've thought of nothing all day but your hot body pressed against mine.' I waited for him to pounce on me, but instead, the lights came on, and I saw that it was Grant's roommate. Red-faced and flustered, he mumbled an apology before turning around and leaving." —Tricia, 22

Love Thy Neighbor

Talk about a wake-up call

"I thought I would surprise my man at his new apartment with breakfast in bed. The door was unlocked, so I went right in, set down the tray on his nightstand, took off my clothes, and quietly slid into bed with him. It felt a little weird because he was taking up so much more room than usual.

"The door was unlocked so I went right in, took off my clothes, and slid into bed...."

Then he rolled over, and I realized I was lying naked next to a stranger! My boyfriend lives in a two-family house and the front doors are next to each other. I'd picked the wrong one! The guy in bed just laughed, but I grabbed my clothes and ran, leaving breakfast behind. Now my guy and his new buddy, the neighbor, joke that I'm the world's best alarm clock." —*Evelyn, 25*

Brotherly Lust

"My fiancé, Dan, and I were staying at my parents' house for the weekend, and we couldn't keep our hands off each other. One night I decided to sneak into his room for a little after-hours hanky-panky. I crawled across the bed and was about to kiss him when I realized it wasn't Dan. Suddenly someone else sat up in bed and screamed. To my total horror, it was my little brother. I'd gone to his room by mistake! I still cringe when I think about it." —*Allison, 26*

64%

OF WOMEN HAVE ACCIDENTALLY PUT THE MOVES ON THE WRONG PERSON..

Footloose

"My boyfriend's father is a minister, and I was nervous about spending an entire weekend at his family's country house. I knew I'd have to be on my absolute best behavior. The first night I was there, my guy could see I was tense when we sat down for dinner, so he started playing footsie with me under the table. Then I slipped off my shoe and placed my foot all the way in his lap, but just as I did, his father jumped up and said, 'This is not a brothel!' I realized then that I'd put my foot in the wrong lap! I was so humiliated that I burst into tears right then and there. My boyfriend tried to explain, but it was too late. My heathen ways were no longer welcome in their home." —*Kathy, 18*

This chick really stepped in it.

Bet she'll be careful where she puts her hands next time

Where's a screen saver when you need one?

I. M. Embarrassed

"I hadn't seen Jason for a week, and I missed him like crazy. One day we started sending racy instant messages to each other. Finally I wrote, 'Baby, I can't wait to have you inside me this weekend.' I expected to get Jason's reply right away, but after a few minutes he still hadn't answered. Then a note popped up on my screen: 'This is Jason's father. He went to shoot hoops with his brothers, but I'll be sure to give him your message.'" —*Sally, 22*

8

Booty Bummer   OH NO!

"Tom and I had spent the night at his parents' house and were getting ready to drive back home. After packing my bag, I was on my way down the hall when I passed Tom as he was bending over. His adorable bubble butt was sticking up in the air, so I spanked him hard and even threw in a full-handed pinch for extra effect. He responded with a little yelp, and I laughed. I then went into the kitchen…where I found Tom, eating a turkey sandwich with his mother. Confused, I glanced back down the hall and realized I'd just goosed Tom's father. I stammered out a quick apology, then buried my face in my hands. Thankfully, his dad started laughing at the whole thing. I guess he appreciated the humor in my little mix-up, but I was totally mortified!"   —*Tanya, 30*

FAUX PAS PROTECTION

Save yourself from a "wrong guy" mishap with these tips.

DON'T I.M. NAUGHTY MESSAGES without conducting a "How do I know it's really you?" interrogation first.

HINT: IF YOU CRAWL INTO a "made" bed (you know, with a top sheet), chances are good it's not your boyfriend's.

IF HE SMELLS LIKE ANOTHER GUY and feels like another guy, he *is* another guy.

EVEN THOUGH HIS ROOMMATE is supposed to be away, pull the elaborate seduction schemes at your place, just in case.

25
LAUGH-OUT-LOUD HILARIOUS TALES

From the dude who got bit in the butt by a duck to the girl who caught her parents getting it on, these stories are so silly, you'll be in stitches.

LAUGH-O-METER

We rated these stories on the funny scale.

YOU'LL SMILE	YOU'LL GIGGLE	YOU'LL CRACK UP	YOU'LL ROLL ON THE FLOOR

"You're walking the dog *now?*"

Mama Drama

"My friends and I were at a bar for happy hour when we noticed this really hot older woman sitting a few tables over. Unfortunately, she was sitting with a couple of men, so we were all afraid to approach her. Finally, she got up to go to the rest room, and when she passed by our table, I stood up, grabbed her around the waist, and asked drunkenly if there was any way she'd be willing to come home with me. First, the woman pushed me away, then she leaned in closer, grabbed my chin, and said, 'William?' As it turned out, it was my mom's friend Raquel, and I was too drunk to recognize her. Luckily, she laughed the whole thing off, said she was flattered, and promised not to say anything to my mother." —Billy, 22

Snoop Dog

"I really liked this girl and finally asked her out on a date. When I went to pick her up at her apartment, she was running late and told me to wait in the living room. She had just gotten a puppy, and while she was getting ready, the new dog came out of the bedroom with something in its mouth. I called the dog's name, and it ran over to me, dropped a pair of the girl's dirty underwear in my lap, and scurried away. I was a little grossed out, but before I had a chance to get rid of them, she stepped out of her bedroom and saw me holding her panties. I explained that her dog had brought them to me, but she looked disgusted and called off our date." —Lennie, 30

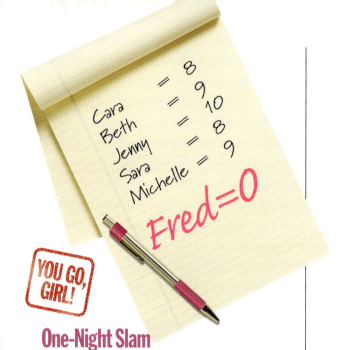

Cara = 8
Beth = 9
Jenny = 10
Sara = 8
Michelle = 9

Fred = 0

YOU GO, GIRL!

One-Night Slam

"My college roommates and I created a rating system for women we'd slept with. Every time one of us would get together with a new girl, we'd assess her bedroom expertise on a scale of 1 to 10 and write it on this master list. We all

> "Every time we got together with a new girl we'd assess her bedroom expertise."

lived in a quad, so we kept the list posted on our refrigerator door. One weekend, I invited this gorgeous girl from my English class back to my dorm to fool around. She got up in the middle of the night to get a glass of water and was taking a long time to come back to bed, so I fell asleep. When I woke up the next morning, I was surprised to see she wasn't there. I stumbled into the kitchen to look for her and found my roommates crowded around our list, laughing. I looked at it and saw that someone had added my name in giant pink cursive with a score of zero." —*Fred, 19*

Dancing Fool

"I know it's not cool for guys to take ballet lessons, but I've done it secretly since I was a kid. Last Christmas, I got busted...big time. Since I was going to be alone on the 24th, I ordered Chinese food, put on my ballet slippers and a leotard, and popped in *The Nutcracker* to practice. A half hour later, there was a knock at my door. I assumed it was the food, but it was my new girlfriend, who dropped by to surprise me, but ended up running away in tears." —*Mark, 23*

Present Tense

"I was trying to make a good impression when I met my ex's parents. Since I knew it was his dad's birthday, I came with a gift: a fancy grooming kit that included a silver razor and soap on a rope. His mom eyed my purchase and said, 'Gee, those are awfully personal. Why don't you just jump into the hot tub with him?' I was mortified, but everyone acted like the woman hadn't said anything unusual." —*Sandi, 24*

She tried to be nice, but wound up hanging herself.

9

"This was not how I wanted him to meet my parents."

Murder to Live With

"My housemate was a real party girl—she would always come home in the wee hours of the morning and crash in the living room. But this one time, she let herself in, stripped off all her clothes, and ate a bunch of corn chips dipped in barbecue sauce before passing out on the couch. The red sauce ended up smeared all over her nude body, and I woke up to hear my boyfriend shouting, 'Linda, there's a dead hooker in the apartment!'" —Linda, 30

"My party-girl housemate passed out on the couch with barbecue sauce smeared all over her naked body."

Stuck at the Scene

"I brought my boyfriend along to spend a weekend at my family's country house. When everyone went out, we stayed behind to get some one-on-one time and began making out on the balcony outside my parents' room. When it started to rain, we moved the action inside. Well, I guess the rain brought my folks home early, because while we were getting busy, we heard them coming up the stairs. With no time to think, we grabbed our clothes and quickly rolled under the bed. Then, my parents came into the room and started going at it themselves! I was about to throw up, but my boyfriend could barely contain his laughter. After my parents finally called it quits and went downstairs, my guy and I snuck out the back door. We returned an hour later and, thankfully, no one asked us where we'd been." —Laureli, 22

After that display, we'd head for the door too.

Buzz Kill

"I went with my roommate to his office happy hour, where I met Brooke, his beautiful coworker. We connected immediately and went on a few dates. One day, Brooke called and said she'd planned a special evening for us. I went over and saw that she'd prepared a candlelight dinner, and I was sure this was going to be 'the night.' All was going well until I saw a bee fly into the room. I'm horribly allergic to bee stings and started shrieking 'Save me! Save me!' Finally, Brooke shooed it out the window. I was hoping we could get back to our date, but Brooke admitted that she was totally turned off at the sight of me screaming like a girl. We never went out again." —Jon, 23

Bathroom Humor

"Before my first big sales presentation at my new job, I went to the bathroom to compose myself. No one was in there, so to get psyched up, I looked in the mirror and said, 'You're great, you'll seal the deal, you're the best, you can do it,' over and over again. When I felt pumped up, I walked out. Standing at the watercooler a few feet away was a crowd of coworkers who'd obviously heard my pep talk. They all laughed and told me I was the greatest." —Maggie, 24

"Our candlelight dinner was going perfectly until I saw a bee fly into the room."

Smack Attack

"I moved into this apartment where a little mouse of a girl had the other bedroom. Her boyfriend was this nerdy guy, and they seemed perfect together. One night, I heard what I thought were threatening noises from behind her closed door: 'I'm going to beat your ass,' he told her. 'Oh, no, help!' she cried. I banged on the door and said I'd call the police if he did not leave my roommate alone. Things got very quiet. 'Um...Liz, it's okay,' she said, and I was like, 'Yeah, right, it's okay. You don't have to be afraid!' I swung the door open and found her in full erotic regalia, a spatula in her guy's hand. I didn't know whether to laugh, apologize, or succumb to the willies." —Liz, 23

This beating was not what it seemed.

She used these socks to stuff, but not where you'd think.

Gender Bender

"Three of my guy friends and I rented a fabulous house for the summer. The only problem was the pesky neighbor who had taken a liking to me and would constantly ask me 'What's crack-a-lackin', gorgeous?' I made it clear that I wasn't interested, but he didn't take the hint. One evening we had a party and, of course, the gross guy showed up. I was talking to friends when he came up behind me and smacked me hard on the butt. That's when I

> ## "I was talking to friends when he smacked me hard on the butt. That's when I finally decided I'd had enough."

finally decided that I'd had enough. Later that night, I stuck a roll of socks in my underwear and pulled him into the bathroom. I pressed myself against him and whispered that I had a secret. Then I took his hand and put it on my crotch to feel the bulge. He ran out of there and never came back to the house again." —Anna, 26

Next time, hold the olives.

All Choked Up

"My friends and I were out at a cocktail lounge when a guy I liked showed up with his friends. As soon as I saw that he was alone, I sauntered over to him with my martini and started flirting. I decided to turn it up a notch, so I put an olive in my mouth and began sucking on it seductively, but I accidentally swallowed it and started choking. The hottie ended up having to give me the Heimlich maneuver in the middle of the bar. After a few tries, the olive flew out of my mouth, and I grunted loudly. I was so flustered that I grabbed my purse and bolted." —*Marla, 31*

S&M Schooling

"I needed to pass physiology in order to graduate from nursing school. During my last semester, knowing I was getting a failing grade, I decided to hit on my sleazy married professor, who had a reputation for returning 'favors.' My professor understood what I was getting at, so he invited me over. To my surprise, when I arrived, he and his wife were waiting for me all decked out in matching leather outfits, sex toys in hand. I quickly changed my mind and booked out of there at lightning speed. I couldn't look my professor in the eye for the rest of the semester, and he seemed equally uncomfortable. I got an A, which I believe had more to do with his embarrassment than my merit." —*Carla, 23*

Butt Quack

"For my second date with Nancy, I wanted to do something special, so I packed a picnic lunch and planned a day at the park. We were sitting by the lake drinking wine, when a family of ducks swam up. After 10 minutes of feeding them bread, we lay down in the grass and took a nap. I was sound asleep when all of a sudden, I felt a sharp pain in my butt. I rolled over and saw one of the ducks biting me and quacking. When Nancy woke up and saw me leaping around holding my rear, saying 'Go away, duck!' she cracked up. To this day, she still teases me about being so 'afwaid of a wittle bitty ducky-wucky.'" —*Scott, 24*

Hope he packed some Band-Aids in this basket

"I was failing miserably, so I decided to hit on my sleazy professor, who had a reputation for returning "favors.""

"Can we just pretend that you didn't see that?"

The Fly's the Limit

"In an effort to impress this girl I'd been dating, I made dinner reservations at a trendy restaurant in our town. It was hard to get a table there, but I called weeks in advance to secure a spot. When we showed up, though, the hostess had no record of my reservation. I demanded to speak to the manager, who told us we would have to wait an hour. I didn't want to look like a chump in front of my date, so I started to lay into him. Since my date seemed to be digging my take-charge attitude, I got even tougher until the manager smiled and said, 'I'm sorry, sir. It'll be an hour. Oh, and by the way, your fly is down.'"

—Matthew, 27

"I wanted to look hot, so I wore my Daisy Dukes, though I really shouldn't have."

Stringing Him Along

"One summer, I went to the boardwalk with a guy I really liked. I was riding the cotton pony, but I wanted to look hot, so I wore my Daisy Dukes anyway. We were sitting on a bench talking when he looked down at my leg and said, 'There's a string hanging out of your shorts.' Then he reached over and tugged at it! I quickly excused myself, saying I had to go find some scissors. Luckily, the guy was clueless and had no idea he'd just given my tampon a hearty tug."

—Lynn, 27

That was one gyno visit she'll never forget.

Boob Blunder

"After a nasty breakup, some friends took me out to drown my sorrows. I ended up having a crazy night and not remembering most of it. A week later, another friend decided I needed more cheering up, so she brought me to the same bar where I'd had my pity party before. The bartender asked if I'd been in last week, and I admitted I'd been there. Then he told me I'd left something behind. That's when he unfolded a bar towel and revealed a silicone cutlet that I'd used to pad my bra. It turns out that in my sad state, I'd announced I wasn't going to pretend to be perfect for any man, whipped out my fake boob, and slammed it onto the bar. Apparently, I'd even asked a few guys if they'd rather date my cutlet or me." —Ellen, 28

Bush Botch Job

"I dressed up as Kelly Osbourne for Halloween one year, so I bought an aerosol can of pink hair color. A couple of days later, I was getting ready for a gynecologist appointment and grabbed a can of feminine deodorant spray. I was running late, so I quickly got dressed and left. But when I got to the gynecologist's office, I was in for quite a surprise. Without realizing it, I'd grabbed the wrong can and had given my pubic hair a hot pink dye job. When I put my feet up in the stirrups, I realized what I'd done and wanted to leave, but just then the doctor came in. He laughed and said, 'Wow, aren't you stylish!'" —Rachel, 32

This chicken won best in show.

WHAT YOUR SENSE OF HUMOR SAYS ABOUT YOU

Take this quiz to find out where you fall on the funny meter.

1 A slimy guy hits on you, saying, "If I told you that you had a good body, would you hold it against me?" You tell him:

a. Why don't you take a shower and get back to me?
b. What a great line! It's hard to believe you're still single.
c. Okay, but are you sure I'll be able to feel anything?

2 You're at a party, about to approach a guy you really like. Just as you get close, you trip and fall flat out in front of him. What's your comeback?

a. Impromptu yoga, anyone?
b. Right about now I'm feeling *damn* sexy.
c. I saved you the trouble of buying me a drink—so go ahead and get on top of me.

3 You're waiting in line at the coffee place when a man asks to cut. You respond:

a. Are you late for etiquette class?
b. Oh right, because I have no place to be.
c. Sure, get in front of me so I can check out your butt.

4 The boss announces major downsizing. The room gets silent, so you chime in with:

a. Do I have to bring back the office supplies I've stolen?
b. Come on, people, we have to save the CEO's yacht!
c. Didn't anyone ever tell you that size *does* matter?

IF YOU ANSWERED MOSTLY A'S, YOU ARE WITTY. You're quick and clever and always armed with a funny comeback. Just be certain you don't keep cracking jokes when people need you to be serious.

IF YOU ANSWERED MOSTLY B'S, YOU ARE SARCASTIC. You point out the irony in a situation by saying one thing when you mean another. Dry humor can seem mean-spirited, so be careful not to offend people.

IF YOU ANSWERED MOSTLY C'S, YOU ARE DIRTY. Everything comes down to sex with you. Your raunchy jokes may get a rise out of your like-minded pals, but just make sure no children or old ladies are around.

SOURCE: JON MACKS, TONIGHT SHOW WRITER AND AUTHOR OF HOW TO BE FUNNY

Maybe he needed another spoonful.

Dopey, Sneezy, Grumpy

"I'd been pursuing Charlotte for months when she finally agreed to go out with me. Unfortunately, a few days before the big night, I came down with a serious cold, so I doped myself up with medicine. Our date was going well, so when I walked her to the door at the end of the evening, I knew a kiss was in the bag. We stood on her porch talking for a while before I took her by the waist and leaned in. Then, without warning, I sneezed right in her face. She screamed and ran into the house. Luckily, she was willing to give me another chance." —Jim, 26

9

"After a wild Saturday night, I left my boyfriend's house, which is right next door to a church...."

Sunday Sinner

"After a wild Saturday night, I left my boyfriend's house, which is right next door to a church. As I trudged down the street in my too-high heels, bird's-nest hair, and smeared lipstick, people were streaming into the church. There was a family in front of me, and the little girl was having a temper tantrum about going to Mass. As I passed by, the girl wailed, 'But she's not going to church!' She was right—I looked like I was going straight to hell." —Erika, 27

She didn't
see that
one coming.

Man in the Middle

"Rick and I had been together for three years, but I had always been attracted to his friend Jake. One night, Jake came over to our apartment to pick up some CDs. Since Rick was out for the evening, I made a move on Jake, and pretty soon we were going at it on the living room couch. Not long afterward, Rick walked in. He screamed 'How could you do this to me?' I quickly jumped up and ran over to him to explain, but he totally ignored me. Instead, his eyes were fixed on his friend. He said to him, 'You told me that if I left her, we could be together!' Apparently, they had been sleeping with each other for months." —*Keri, 23*

"Suddenly, it was just too quiet and I had a panic attack. I shoved all my books off the table and started screaming."

Finals Frenzy

"College library, freshman year, finals. Everyone was nose-to-the-books in a state of mad anxiety, studying. It was 2 a.m. in a vast room full of crammers. The total silence added to my tension, and the four cups of coffee I'd had since dinner didn't help either. Suddenly, it was just too quiet, and I had a major panic attack. I shoved all my books off the table and started screaming 'I can't take it anymore! I can't take it anymore!' I ran out of the library, knocking over books left and right with my backpack on the way out. I don't know what possessed me. It was a big school, so I didn't think I'd see any of those people again, but guess what? By senior year, everyone was referring to me as 'that girl who lost it in the library.'" —*Karen, 27*

Meat Head

"After going out on a few dates with Mandy, we ended up back at her place. After fooling around for a while, I went into her kitchen for something to drink. Inside her fridge was a whole steak, just sitting there. I hadn't eaten much dinner and was ravenous, so I devoured about half of it. When I crawled back into bed 20 minutes later, Mandy asked why I smelled like steak sauce. I told her I'd eaten the meat in the fridge and offered to take her out to dinner the following night to make up for it. She then burst into hysterical laughter. When I asked what was so funny, she told me that the steak was raw—she'd been marinating it overnight. I started freaking out. I even called my mom to ask if I should go to the hospital to have my stomach pumped. My mother eased my fears a bit, but she demanded that I put Mandy on the phone. While I sat there in bed, embarrassed beyond belief, my mom proceeded to tell Mandy not to let me anywhere near her refrigerator again." —Steven, 28

This guy got a raw deal.

All she had to do was ask.

Name Shame

"After spending the night with a guy I'd just met, I couldn't remember his name. I liked him, so I didn't want to get caught going through his wallet for his ID. Instead, I asked him to write down his number so I could call him. But he failed to include his name on the paper. Thinking I was being sly, I asked if he could spell his name for me. He gave me a look, then said, 'B-I-L-L.'" —Judy, 27

9

"After spending the night with a guy I'd just met, I realized I couldn't remember his name."

Cheese Fond-eeew!

"I'd finally snagged a date with my supersexy neighbor. I really wanted to impress her, so I made a reservation at a cozy Italian restaurant. When we got to dinner, I ordered a bottle of wine and apps while we looked over the menu. I was starving, so when the mozzarella sticks came, I dug right in. Suddenly, I started choking on the cheese. I was gagging, and my date screamed for someone to come help us. Finally, I reached into the back of my mouth and pulled out the cheese. It came out, but I still threw up all over the table." —Charlie, 32

CAUGHT IN THE ACT BY THE COPS

Getting busted mid-booty is bad enough, but when the police nab you in a naughty position... now that's really a crime.

"We're going to have to write you up for indecent exposure."

Pool Patrol

"I'd been dating Chris for six months when he asked me to fly home with him to Texas to meet his parents. Our first night there was warm and humid, so we went skinny-dipping in his pool at midnight. We started kissing, and soon we were getting busy on the stairs in the shallow end. I must have been making a lot of noise because the next thing we knew, two cops were standing at the edge of the pool and yelling at us to get out. Apparently, his parents had heard our commotion and called the police, thinking someone was trying to break in. We scrambled to get out of the pool, and I had to walk past his parents completely bare chested. The next morning Chris's mom took me aside and told me that I should stay at a hotel because I was no longer welcome in her house."
—Jamie, 20

Strip Search

"I was in Las Vegas for a long weekend, and I met this hottie, Jay. We had to get creative about finding spots to hook up, though, since we were both rooming with friends. On our last night, we were walking down the Strip when we saw a stage that was closed for renovations. So we ducked behind the curtain and went at it. Things were getting pretty heated when the curtain suddenly flew open. Everyone at the bar turned to see, thinking that a show had started. We grabbed our clothes and ran to the side of the stage, where a security guard was waiting to escort us out."
—Emily, 30

Looks almost as messy as the sitch she got herself in

Love Don't Cost a Sting

"My boyfriend Brett was coming home for Christmas break, so I went to pick him up from the airport. I hadn't seen him in months, and I wanted to look supersexy, so I wore a really skimpy outfit and red lipstick. On the way home we couldn't keep our hands off each other, so I finally pulled into an alley. Just as we were finishing, a cop on a motorcycle pulled up beside us and ordered us to get out of the car. Apparently, he thought I was a streetwalker! It took us 20 minutes to explain the situation, but once we did, the cop was more embarrassed than me." —Heather, 21

"The officer came up to the car window and asked what was hanging around my neck...."

Cops and Rubbers

"Kyle, my boyfriend, and I were parked in an empty lot, hooking up in the backseat of his car, when three police cars came screeching up. They surrounded us with their lights flashing, and the cops shouted at us to get out. Although we were half naked, they forced us to put our hands in the air while they searched through our stuff. As it turned out, Kyle's car was the same model as one being driven by some men who'd just robbed a liquor store. Once we cleared things up, the cops jokingly offered to start a collection for us at the station so we could get a real room." —Anna, 24

Pantie Police

"My girlfriend was driving us home from a wedding when I started feeling horny. The road was pretty deserted, so I decided to give her some oral pleasure. She was wearing a skirt, and she managed to slip off her thong by alternating her legs on the pedals. Everything was great...until a police car pulled up behind us and flashed its lights. My girlfriend stopped the car, and we quickly adjusted ourselves. The cop came up to the window and asked me what was hanging around my neck. I assumed he meant my bow tie, so I said as much. Then the officer pulled on it and said, 'Son, that doesn't look like a tie to me!' I looked down to discover that my girlfriend's pink thong was hanging around my neck." —Steve, 32

At least they can laugh about it now.

WHAT NOT TO SAY TO THE COPS

"Would you mind frisking us again? It felt great."

"You're obviously not getting any or else you'd understand."

"Could you give us a few more minutes? We're almost finished."

Prisoner of Love

The things some people do for love…

"My fiancée's overprotective parents used to hate me so much that they threatened to disown her if she continued dating me. We had to start seeing each other on the sly. Since she still lived with them at the time, I used to scale two stories to her window late at night. One time her neighbors spotted me and called the police. My girlfriend was so afraid of her folks that she wouldn't tell the truth to the cops. I was arrested for trespassing and ended up spending a night in jail. She's lucky I love her so much." —Robert, 25

"And I thought the only action I'd see would be high-speed car chases."

10

CARNAL CRACKDOWNS

Laugh all you want, but these weird anti-lust laws are actually on the books…even if they're not enforced.

IN **UTAH**, it's illegal to have oral sex.

IN **OKLAHOMA**, it's illegal to seduce a virgin by promising that you'll marry her.

IN **SOUTH CAROLINA**, it's illegal for any unmarried man or woman to "make a habit" of engaging in sexual intercourse.

IN **INDIANA**, it's illegal for a man to have a visible erection in public, even if it is covered by clothing.

SOURCES: *A GUIDE TO AMERICA'S SEX LAWS* BY JUDGE RICHARD A. POSNER AND KATHARINE B. SILBAUGH; STATE CRIMINAL CODES

Bound and Gagged

NAUGHTY, NAUGHTY!

"My guy Brian and I were going through a really wild phase, and we wanted to get a little frisky alfresco. I'd always dreamed of acting out a crazy fantasy I had about being a prisoner, so one night Brian took some rope and tied me to a picnic table by a lake. We were right in the thick of things when a bright light suddenly blinded me. It was a forest ranger. When he saw me lying naked and tied up on the table, he started screaming for Brian to back away from me. After a lot of explaining, we finally convinced him that it was all part of a sexual role-play." —Denise, 28

When this couple ties the knot, it isn't what you think.

"DURING A WAXING SESSION, YOU'RE BOUND TO FIND YOURSELF IN SOME VERY COMPROMISING POSITIONS."

CONFESSIONS OF

A Bikini Waxer

A woman who spends her day doing Brazilians breaks her code of silence. Listen in as she spills cringe-worthy client discoveries.

■ Even if you haven't yet braved a Brazilian bikini wax, you've probably wondered what it's like. The Brazilian requires you to get naked from the waist down and lie spread-eagle on a table while an aesthetician smears hot wax on your pubic hair and rips it off, except for a tiny patch. Or, if you request, you can go even further and have it all removed.

One thing is guaranteed: During a Brazilian bikini wax, you're bound to find yourself in some very compromising positions. I'm a professional waxer, and I've seen some wacky things, like the woman who brought in her boyfriend and wanted me to wax him while she watched. But I have much more to tell, including kinky client gossip, why my job can be dangerous, and the secret about a strange customer I hope I'll never see again.

Waxed to the Max

Five years ago, I enrolled in a cosmetology school to learn the trade. I'd always loved giving friends facials and helping them with beauty problems, and by going to school, I could make a living doing what I enjoy most.

In about six months, I earned my aesthetician's license, which included training in doing facials and hair removal. Immediately afterward, I began to work at an upscale salon as a waxer. I didn't do Brazilians back then—in fact, I'd never even heard of them because they weren't popular yet in the States.

But a few years ago, a friend suggested that I go to her aesthetician for a new kind of sexy, "thorough" wax. "It's called a Brazilian," she said. "It's how women from Brazil do it so they can wear their G-strings on the beach and look perfect." It sounded good to me. But little did I know what looking "perfect" entailed.

I got to the woman's salon, took off my pants, and hopped on the table as usual. When she asked me to take off my underwear, I was hesitant, to say the least. But I agreed, figuring this was what my friend goes through. I was too embarrassed to look at what she was doing, so I just stared up at the ceiling. Suddenly, I felt her putting wax on the hair on my vaginal lips. Before I could react, she yanked it off. It hurt like hell, and I was tempted to ask her to stop. But I was intrigued, so I let her go on.

Confessions of a Bikini Waxer

I actually started to look down and watch her technique carefully, so I could learn how to do it myself. But when she asked me to lift my legs up and spread my butt cheeks, I wished I could throw my clothes on and run.

Finally it was over, and she gave me a mirror to check out her handiwork. I liked it! The whole area felt so smooth and soft, and it was cool to see what my private parts really looked like! But the best was when my boyfriend saw it. He'd never been with a totally "bald" woman before; he said, "My God, you're so hot!" and couldn't get enough of me.

I learned some more technique tips from the aesthetician. Then I convinced my sister, whom I always wax, to be my guinea pig so that I could practice. She didn't want to go through with it at first, especially when I told her I'd be removing her butt-crack hair! But her husband overheard me trying to talk her into it and said, "Come on, try it. It sounds really sexy." She reluctantly agreed. My sis handled the pain fairly well (only cursing at me once or twice), and she was completely ecstatic with the results, as was her husband. Soon after, I turned my clients on to the bare look. Now everyone, including my sister, is totally addicted to it.

Coping With Kooky Customers

After looking at people's privates for so long, I've seen more shapes, sizes, and hair-growth patterns than you can imagine. One customer came in look-

Bring on the pain!

ing perfectly put together, but when she undressed, I could see hair extending halfway down her thigh and all the way up her stomach. It looked like a small carpet! I thought, *Where am I going to start?* I spent nearly two hours getting all that hair off.

Another client likes to jog in for a Brazilian after working out at the gym. She doesn't seem to understand that the odor can be incredibly strong if you don't wash first (which most of my customers do with a bit of wet tissue in the salon's bathroom). So I have to ask her to use a baby wipe before I go near her. Thankfully, most of my clients have much better hygiene than that chick.

A lot of women like to use their bikini areas as a canvas for artistic expression, like the one who asked me to prune her pubic hair into the shape of a heart, which she planned to dye pink. Ironically, I've found that the more conservative a customer looks, the kinkier she tends to be. There's a successful lawyer who comes in for her monthly appointment dressed in designer suits and classy pumps. No one would

PRETTY BOYS

No wonder guys these days look so damn good. According to the International Spa Association, men now comprise almost 30 percent of all spa-goers, which explains services like the "boyzilian" wax (a Brazilian for men) and the "love handles body wrap."

'ONE OF MY CLIENTS THRASHES AROUND SO VIOLENTLY THAT I'M AFRAID SHE'S GOING TO BREAK THE TABLE."

guess she has a butterfly tattoo below her hipbone and a pierced clitoris. One prim housewife told me that she had to make sure her "love muffin was picture-perfect" because she and her husband like to swing. She wanted to look good for him and the other guys who were going to see her naked that weekend.

A few of my clients are even dangerous. One woman thrashes around so violently from the pain that I'm afraid she's going to break the table and spill hot wax all over both of us. She'll kick her legs, rip the paper table cover, throw towels, and scream at the top of her lungs, "Damn you! That hurts!" When it's over, she gives me a hug and says, "See you in a month."

The Creepiest Client Ever

I had my strangest waxing experience with a woman who actually liked being on the receiving end. The first time I began waxing her, her skin was really wet. I thought it was just nervous perspiration, so I put powder over the area to keep her dry so the wax would stick. But it wasn't working; she continued to get soaked, and I suddenly realized she was getting turned on! I was so freaked out, I wanted to tell her to leave. But I had a job to do, so I finished it as quickly as I could just to get her out of there with minimal embarrassment.

I agreed to see her again one month later, hoping I'd been mistaken, but I wasn't. Clearly, she was enjoying herself a bit too much. She had a dreamy expression on her face and was nibbling on her finger like she was fantasizing. Afterward, she paid and left without a word. Thankfully, she hasn't come back since, the weirdo.

Despite the occasional oddball, I've developed an excellent rapport with most of my clients. They trust me, and I feel great when they tell me how much they appreciate my handiwork. At this point, there's no cosmetic request that I find too shocking or strange to accommodate. After all, as the woman who wanted her pubic hair shaped like an arrow pointing down, with little crystals spelling out "Slippery When Wet" can probably attest, beauty is all in the eye of the beholder. ∎

"MY WHACKED-OUT WAXING EXPERIENCE"

After reading these terrible tales, you might opt for laser hair removal.

"To prepare for a big date, I got myself waxed for the first time. The wax really burned, but I assumed that was normal. But when my date reached up my skirt, he found my entire bikini area covered in red blisters!" —Stacy, 23

"I agreed to let the new girl at the salon do my bikini wax for half the price. She hadn't mastered the art because not only did it hurt like hell, but when I got home, there were still clumps of wax in all the remaining hair, sticking like chewing gum." —Candace, 27

"I used to shave my bikini line, and I'd get in-grown hairs. I finally decided I needed a wax. It was painful, but she did a good job…in fact, too good. She spent 45 minutes taking out each ingrown hair with tweezers." —Joanna, 31

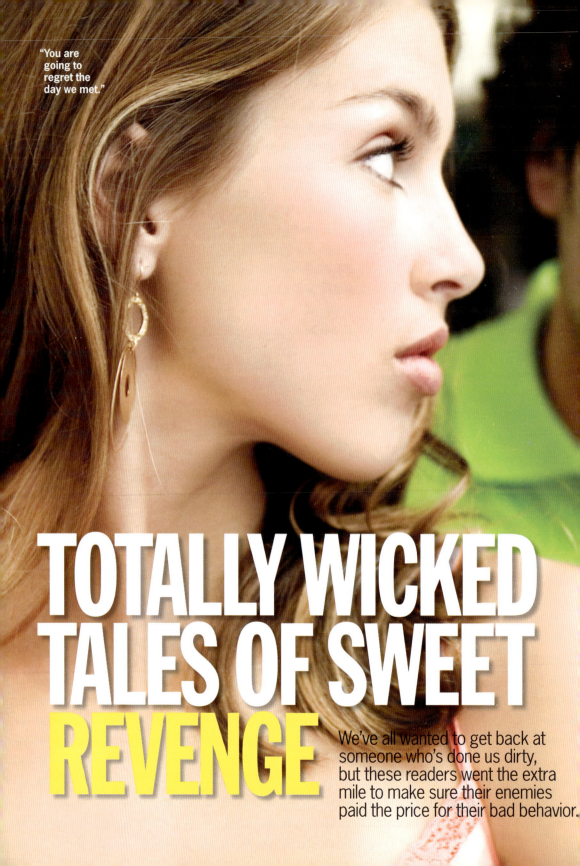

11

"You are going to regret the day we met."

TOTALLY WICKED TALES OF SWEET REVENGE

We've all wanted to get back at someone who's done us dirty, but these readers went the extra mile to make sure their enemies paid the price for their bad behavior.

Livin' La Vida Loser

"I found out that one of my competitive coworkers, Bill, was bashing me behind my back and constantly telling my boss that I was slacking off on the job. After two months of putting up with his crap, I decided to get revenge. I knew the boss was coming into Bill's office for an early meeting the next morning, so before Bill arrived at work, I sneaked into his office with a bunch of Ricky Martin paraphernalia. I then covered his walls with Ricky Martin posters and replaced all the photos in his frames with pics of Ricky. Later on, when I was walking by his office, I overheard our boss saying, 'Wow, Bill, you're really living la vida loca, aren't you?' Everyone found out about his little fetish, and a week later at an office party, someone brought a cardboard cutout of Ricky Martin to give to Bill. He looked totally embarrassed."
—Kevin, 23

12

Fake-Out Phone Call

"When I caught my boyfriend cheating on me, I thought the best way to get back at him was to teach him about the benefits of monogamy. I had my sister Julie call his skank-on-the-side and identify herself as a social worker from the public health office. Julie then explained to the little home-wrecker that a man they'd just treated for herpes had listed her as a sex partner, so she'd better get herself checked out—and inform her lovers, who were infected and spreading the disease to anyone they'd been with. You should have seen my boyfriend squirm at dinner with me that night when I mentioned my (made-up) gyno appointment the next day."
—Shelby, 22

You can't have your cake and eat it too.

Just Desserts

"My girlfriend Sheila decided to throw a huge party for her parents' 25th anniversary. It was about that time that I learned she had been sleeping around on me. My first instinct was to dump her right away, but then I had a better idea. It was my job

"When I found out my girlfriend was sleeping around behind my back, I got an evil idea...."

to pick up the big, beautiful sheet cake for the party. Instead of driving it right to her parents' place, I used a tube of frosting to write on it 'Congrats on your anniversary. Too bad Sheila and I won't be having one since she's such a slut!' Then I left it on the kitchen table and took off." —Brad, 23

HAVE YOU PUBLICLY HUMILIATED SOMEONE BECAUSE YOU WERE TICKED OFF?

54% OF WOMEN SAID YES.

52% OF MEN SAID YES.

Bad Medicine

NAUGHTY, NAUGHTY!

"I am an assistant to the chief of staff at a hospital, and one summer, I had to work alongside his teenage daughter. She was a spoiled brat who was always gabbing on her cell phone. When I overheard her tell a friend she'd just swiped prescription pills, I decided to bust her. I secretly cut a slit in the bottom of her bag, so when she picked it up, a ton of packets fell out, right in front of several doctors. She was fired on the spot." —Greg, 29

Just add water, and it's a hot tub on wheels.

Hose Job

"Stephen and I had a horrible breakup. To make matters worse, the girl he started dating lived next door to me, so I always saw them together. One day, he had the nerve to park in my driveway when he came to see her. I was out getting the mail when I noticed that his passenger window was open. Somehow, my garden hose found its way into his car, spraying water all over the upholstery. The best part was that nothing looked wet, so when they sat down, their behinds got drenched. Even from my bathroom upstairs, I could hear them swearing at me. Now, they meet at Stephen's place instead." —Katherine, 20

Yikes! Wouldn't want to get on *his* bad side

Spaghetti O-No!

"When my best friend, Ken, and his girlfriend moved in together, they decided to have a dinner party. A week before the event, I found out that Ken had slept with my girlfriend. To get back at him, I decided to wreak havoc at his party. On my way over, I picked up some worms from a bait shop and stuck them in a plastic bag in my pocket. While I was helping

"She screamed, 'How am I supposed to get out of here without cash or clothes?'"

Ken's girlfriend with dinner, I dropped the worms into the spaghetti I was tossing. We sat down to eat, and midway through the meal, Ken started screaming. All of the worms had made it into his dish! He gagged, then vomited all over his new rug." —*Max, 26*

Room Diss-Service

"When I got my credit-card bill and saw that my girlfriend had run up a $15,000 bill, I flipped out. We had planned a trip to Seattle for the following weekend, so I decided to hold off on confronting her. Our first night in the hotel, I raided the minibar and ordered a full-course dinner for us from room servce. That night while she was sleeping, I took all of her stuff, including her clothes, her cell phone, and *my* credit card, got in my car, and drove back home, leaving her stranded with a huge hotel bill to pay. The next morning, she called me in hysterics from the room. She screamed 'How am I supposed to get myself out of here without cash or clothes?' I suggested she apply for her own credit card and charge it." —*Joshua, 32*

DO NOT DISTURB!

12

Behave badly, and it's gonna cost you

Floppy Diss

"My writing professor was a total jerk who would slam my stories in class, but then steal some of my ideas for his own work. I was sick of his attacks, so one afternoon, I went to visit him during office hours to talk. When I got there, he was closing up his laptop, bragging about the fact that he was almost finished with his novel. That gave me an idea. As I was about to sit down in his chair, I accidentally spilled my huge bottle of water all over his

"I was sick of his attacks, so one day, I went to visit him during office hours to talk."

computer. The screen immediately went blank, and my professor literally started screaming, 'Nooooo!' The best part was that the disk he was using to back up his work was inside his computer at the time, and that got ruined too." —*Tracy, 32*

Dirty Money

"After wondering why my guy was logging in so many late hours at work, I found out that he was sleeping with a coworker. I wasn't going to let any woman get away with stealing my man, so I took a hundred one-dollar bills and wrote the woman's name, phone number, and 'Call me for great head' on each one. I used them all right away, and I'm sure the tramp's phone was ringing off the hook." —*Candace, 27*

COSMO'S PAYBACK PRIMER

When you're exacting revenge, there's a right way and a *sooo* wrong way to go about it.

CRIME	OKAY	EVIL
Your boyfriend cheats on you.	You spread the word that lover boy is a sleaze.	You spread the word that he has herpes.
Your friend keeps borrowing your clothes.	You help yourself to the contents of her closet.	You have a garage sale and sell her stuff.
A friend messes around with your ex.	You track down her ex and make out with him.	You track down her ex and marry him.

Bad-Girl Branding

"I found out my girlfriend had been cheating on me, so I decided to do some permanent damage to punish her for my broken heart. I'm a tattoo artist, so one night, I begged her to let me do her name on her lower back. Well, instead of branding her with ANNA, I tattooed SLUT on her instead. As soon as I finished, she went to check it out in the mirror. The moment she started screaming, I ran for it." —Jacob, 27

Tough luck, Goldilocks!

They're smiling on the outside, fuming on the inside.

Shear Madness

"My sister used to climb all over my fiancé, claiming it was innocent flirting. She was going over the top, though. One night she got so tipsy that she fell asleep on the sofa, but not before trying to kiss my man. So I took her home in her semiconscious state, grabbed a pair of scissors, and chopped off her hair. When she woke up the next day and saw that her long blond hair was gone, she freaked. I told her she had insisted on doing it in her drunken stupor, and I couldn't get the scissors away from her because she was waving them around like a maniac. Now, she looks so bad, she keeps away from men—including mine." —Sara, 26

Cashing Out `12`

"A friend of mine said that when he was out with my girlfriend one night, she hit on him. After confirming the info, I decided to exact revenge. My birthday was coming, so when she asked me what I wanted, I mentioned a pricey stereo system I'd been eyeing. On the night of my birthday, she gave me the gift. Then we went to dinner, where I ordered a $120 bottle of wine, caviar, and the lobster entrée. After my girlfriend paid, I thanked her for a wonderful birthday. Then in front of the entire restaurant, I told her I never wanted to see her again." —Travis, 24

27% OF GUYS HAVE SPREAD RUMORS ABOUT AN EX TO GET BACK AT HER.

Cheap Shot

"I agreed to be a bridesmaid in a friend's wedding, so I threw her a bachelorette party and wound up paying $250 for a dress. A month before the event, she decided she needed to have a more economical event and cut out all the bridesmaids from the ceremony. She also told me that I could come to the wedding, but the reception was for family only. I couldn't get my money back for the dress, and the bride-to-be wouldn't shell out a dime. Luckily, when I got engaged, I was able to get back at her. I told her my wedding was going to be in Hawaii and said she had better book her ticket early so the seats wouldn't sell out. I waited until two weeks before the date to tell her that the ceremony was really in my hometown (less than a hundred miles away)." —Helena, 31

Cheer up, dude. Think of all the fun you'll have at Halloween parties.

Gold Digger

"I went to meet my fiancé at a bar after work and found him making out with a friend of mine. We got into a huge screaming match. The bartender told us to take it outside, so we continued our brawl on the curb. My guy then told me that he'd never been in love with me in the first place and asked for the engagement ring back. I was so pissed that I pulled it off my finger, threw it down the sewer grate, and told him to go fetch it. What a delight it was to watch him clamber down into that smelly abyss in his expensive designer suit and tie!" —Natasha, 24

SOOO EVIL! Hair of the Dog

"When I found out my guy lied to me about getting a lap dance from a stripper, I was willing to forgive him, but he needed to be punished. One night, he came home sick from work and took some cold medicine, so I knew he'd be out like a light. I undressed him and covered his 'bikini area' with hair remover. I let it sit while I watched a movie, then wiped it off. His hip-to-thigh region was totally bare. But I'd left the cream on so long, he'd developed a rash. The next morning, he frantically called me into the shower to see his below-the-belt baldness. I said it looked like an STD a friend of mine had had. The scare was enough to keep him from straying again." —Dana, 21

This is one scene she didn't want to see.

On the Down-Load

"After dating Mariah for six months, a good friend forwarded me digital pics of her swapping spit with another guy. I was furious and decided to get even. We were long-distance, so sometimes we would use our Web cams to strip for each other. One evening, I invited an old fling over. Before she arrived, I called

'I set up a Web cam, then called my girlfriend and told her I had a surprise...."

Mariah and told her that she should leave her Web cam on, and I'd have a kinky surprise for her later. I then pointed my Web cam directly at my bed, and when my ex arrived, we did the deed for an hour. Mariah was watching the entire thing." —*Seth, 31*

Brownie Points

"I stayed at my boyfriend's place so much that I started to buy groceries. But his roommates were constantly helping themselves to my food despite my pleas not to touch it. I got so fed up that I baked a batch of brownies using eggs and butter that had been in the back of the fridge for years. Then I covered the goodies with frosting and put them out with a note that read 'Hands off!' My guy and I went to bed early, but I heard his roommates come home around midnight and start chowing. The next morning, I overheard one of them pounding on the bathroom door and yelling, 'Man, let me in! I *really* gotta go!' Neither one of them ever found out." —*Carol, 25*

Do your own damn grocery shopping!

12

She's plotting a presentation her class will actually pay attention to.

YOU GO, GIRL!

A Member-able Moment

"In college, I dated a guy from my art history class, but we broke up after two months because he said he couldn't handle a relationship. A week later, I discovered he had been talking smack about me. I was furious, so I created a plan to get revenge. He happens to have an oddly shaped penis, and I drew a picture of it and made it into a slide. Underneath the sketch, I wrote his name and a detailed description of his less-than-stellar skills in the sack. When class started, my professor turned on the projector and the embarrassing info was on the big screen for everyone to see! My ex was so traumatized, he ran out of the room and dropped the class later that semester." —Jackie, 23

You've Got Voice Mail

"A few months ago, my fiancée, Brooke, and I broke off our engagement, and she moved out. Unbeknownst to me, she was still calling in to check our voice mail. One day when I was home, I caught her, so I decided to play a little trick. I had a female friend leave a message saying what a great time she'd had with me last night and how she couldn't wait for our trip to Tahiti. Brooke called me in hysterics, screaming at me for taking another chick on 'our' honeymoon. That'll teach her not to snoop." —Mark, 28

"I found out my ex was checking my voice mail, so I decided to play a little trick on her."

Ex-Terminator

"My ex and I had been together for five years when, one day, he told me he didn't love me anymore and had met someon else who he thought was The One. Not only that, but I had three days to get my stuff out of his house so that she could move in. Well, I spent the next two days in tears while I packed boxes. But by the third day, I was ready to fight back. I went to a local pet store, bought 50 baby rats, and let them all go free in his place. I considered it a housewarming gift to his new chick. Hopefully that cheating rat learned his lesson!" —Melissa, 25

Cut Down to Size

"When my college roommate started planning her wedding, she went nuts. After six months of her being so self-absorbed that she never even asked about my sick mother, I couldn't deal with it anymore. I finally got back at her when she asked me to pick up her dress from the alterations shop. I talked the tailor into taking it in another half-inch at the waist because the bride had dropped some weight. In reality, she had put on a couple of pounds. When she got the dress, she couldn't zip it up and went on a crazy juice fast. The day of the wedding, she looked like a huge sausage and could barely breathe." —Ayesha, 27

One man + one computer = trouble.

Racy Report

"I made the mistake of working freelance for a friend who was starting a new company. Instead of being up-front about the fact that his business was not doing well, he lied and kept saying things were great. After my second paycheck bounced, he stopped taking

12

"I logged on to my friend's e-mail and sent a pic to his clients they'd never forget."

my calls. For weeks, I tried to track him down, but he had disappeared. I really wanted to get back at him, and then I remembered the password to his e-mail account. I logged on as him and under the subject line 'Bimonthly Report,' I forwarded a porn shot of a skanky woman to all of his clients." —Tom, 24

49% OF WOMEN HAVE GOTTEN REVENGE ON AN EX.

"So, what are you wearing?"

"My boss was a total chump, so I enlisted my friends to help me get him fired...."

Carnal Conference Call

"My boyfriend goes to college in another state, so we have phone sex to keep the spark alive. One night when he called, my friends were hanging out in my room. I was pissed at him for not calling all week, but I pretended that I was in the mood for some long-distance lovin'. I put him on speakerphone so all of my friends could hear him. Just as he was about to finish, we burst out laughing. He was mortified." —Kaisha, 20

OOPS! Bride Basher

"I'm an editor at a small-town newspaper, and one of my responsibilities is to edit the wedding announcements. When I found out that my younger sister's worst enemy from high school was getting married, I thought it would be funny to write a dummy announcement that read 'The bride-to-be is unemployed and pregnant, and this is her third marriage.' I gave it to my sister as a joke. But somehow, the piece ended up running in the paper! The poor bride was humiliated, so I explained that someone must have sent in the wrong information as a prank." —Melanie, 29

Mall Rat

"I work at a clothing store in the mall, and one of my supervisors was a total chump. He always yelled at me in front of the staff about stupid stuff like not folding the sleeves of the shirts at an exact 90-degree angle and forgetting to coordinate complementary colors when I was laying out the merchandise. One day, after he made me go on a fourth coffee run for him, I'd had it. That night, I asked five of my pals to call up, pretend to be irate customers, and complain about my supervisor. I even had my friend claim the guy tried to peep through her dressing-room door while she was changing. My crappy boss was fired four days later." —Christine, 24

"Let's see: What's the best way to make the idiot suffer?"

It's hard to stay angry at a boy with a face like that.

A Psychic for a Psycho

The crystal ball predicts trouble ahead.

"When my unfaithful girlfriend Elizabeth and I broke up, she went crazy. One night, she called me in a drunken haze, screaming. I told her to go to bed and hung up. A few minutes later, the phone rang again. When I picked it up, I could hear numbers being dialed. Finally, Elizabeth sobbed, 'Is this the psychic hot line?' She had accidentally hit redial while trying to call a 900 number. I realized that this was my opportunity to get rid of her. I disguised my voice and pretended to be a phone psychic. When she asked if she would ever get back together with her ex, I advised her that if she stopped calling him, he would come crawling back to her. Elizabeth must have bought it because she stopped stalking me after that."

—Bobby, 24

Blond Bombshell

12

"After dating this guy for two years, my best friend found out he'd been cheating on her. I went to high school with the other girl and thought she was a skank. One day, the sleazy girl showed up at the salon I work at. I hated this chick for doing my friend wrong, so when the colorist was mixing her dye, I slipped some extra peroxide into the mixture. The girl's locks turned white, and she got a rash on her scalp. She was hysterical, and it took the colorist two hours to get her mane to look normal again."

—Katie, 21

38% OF GUYS HAVE GOTTEN BACK AT A CHEATING GIRLFRIEND.

EXCRUCIATING
EX-BOYFRIEND
ENCOUNTERS

Running into a former flame is rarely fun, but when you're having a bad day to begin with, it can be downright torturous. Wait till you read what happened when these chicks bumped into an old beau.

If you see this guy coming, run the other way.

Treadmill Trauma

"I hadn't been to the gym in ages, but I dragged myself there one night after work. A mere five minutes into my workout, I was already gasping for breath. Just as I was about to slow down my jog to a walk, a guy climbed on the treadmill next to me. I glanced over and realized that it was Ben, the guy who'd dumped me two months earlier. I nodded hello and then cranked up the speed because I was hell-bent on not letting him see how unfit I was. Almost immediately my legs got rubbery, I felt nauseous, and I thought I might faint. I had to push the emergency stop button on the machine, sit down on the end of the belt, and put my head between my legs. Of course Ben stopped his workout to see what was wrong with me. As if it wasn't bad enough to be hyperventilating in front of him, a trainer had to help me to the locker room." —Sally, 28

13

No Day at the Beach

"My boyfriend and I had a wicked breakup last summer, and I decided a shopping spree at a discount store would make me feel better. I rolled out of bed, threw on a ratty college tee shirt and cutoffs, and headed out. I strolled up and down the aisles, stocking up on everything in sight—from bulk boxes of tampons to jumbo canisters of licorice. With my cart overflowing, I strolled over to the sporting-goods section. Right as I turned down the aisle, I bumped into my ex and his new beautiful blond girlfriend. He told me they were buying stuff to take to the beach that day—and his girlfriend had the gall to ask me if I wanted to 'tag along.' I felt like the biggest loser on the planet, spending a beautiful summer Saturday tampon shopping." —Patricia, 26

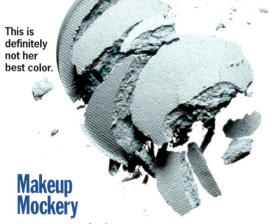

This is definitely not her best color.

Makeup Mockery

"My cousin asked me to be in her wedding, and she thought it would be fun if all the bridesmaids had their makeup done for a trial run a few weeks before the event. Against my will, I sat there and let the makeup artist cover my eyes in electric blue eye shadow, 'contour' my cheeks with brown rouge, and stain my lips bright pink. I looked like a cross between a hooker and a beauty-pageant contestant. I couldn't wait to get home and wash the stuff off. Naturally, I ran into my ex on the way out of the mall. He was so shocked by my appearance that the first words out of his mouth were, 'You look so different!' I tried to explain why I looked like a freak, but the damage had already been done." —*Nadia, 28*

Walk of Shame

"When my boyfriend broke up with me I was really upset. Still, I hoped that he would change his mind and we would get back together. To cheer me up, some of my friends took me out for a night on the town. Well, I started flirting like crazy with one of my guy friends, who just happened to live in my ex's apartment complex. I ended up going home

"I started flirting with one of my guy friends, who just happened to live in my ex's apartment complex."

with him, which was stupid. In the morning I tried to sneak out early to avoid bumping into my ex. As luck would have it, though, we ran into each other the second I walked out the door. He went into a rage and screamed at me so loudly, it woke the neighbors. I knew at that moment that there was no way we'd be getting back together." —*Justine, 30*

WHAT TO SAY WHEN YOU SEE YOUR EX

The next time you cross paths with him, slip one of these lines into the conversation:

"Sorry I look like such a mess, but I spent the night at my boyfriend's and forgot my blow-dryer at home."

"Hi, it's good to see you! I haven't thought about you in *so* long."

"I've been doing a lot of yoga since we split and I'm really limbering up."

"Hey Jim, I mean John....Oh my God, I can't believe I forgot your name like that!"

"Rick...Mark...
Rick...Mark..."

No Ex-planation Necessary

"Rick and I split up after I cheated on him with my friend Mark. He was furious with me even though I told him that the hookup was only a one-time fling. Mark and I stayed friends, and several months later he and I went to lunch together. We were sitting at a table outside, looking like a couple, when Rick walked up. I was still feeling guilty about my cheating and didn't want him to get the wrong impression, so I started stammering to Rick that Mark and I were just friends. But he said, 'Please. Don't be so arrogant. I got over you a long time ago, and I couldn't care less about who you share your bed with now.' I was speechless as I watched him walk away." —*Melissa, 31*

Phone Flub

"I was home from college over a holiday break and heard about a huge party that my ex-boyfriend Rob was having. The night of the big bash, I was on the phone in my room with my friend Amy, analyzing in detail whether or not I should go. After a good 10 minutes of this, I heard an 'ahem,' turned around, and saw Rob standing there. My mom had let him in and told him to head right up to my room. I could tell from the look on his face that he'd heard everything. As I stood there blushing, he launched into a singsong, girlie-voiced imitation of my convo: 'I could totally go, but then again, it could, like, suck.' There was no way to recover." —*Caroline, 22*

Proof these two were once a happy couple

13

Best Laid Plans

"My ex-boyfriend Ron ended up dumping me after I gained weight. Immediately afterward I started going to the gym regularly and eating right, and after three months, I looked amazing. I wanted to rub my ex's face in it, so I asked him to dinner. The day before our date I made an appointment to get a facial, blow-out, and wax, and even bought a new outfit. When Ron saw me, his jaw dropped. After dinner we went back to my place, but in spite of all my planning, I had completely forgotten to shave my legs, and they were hairy as hell! Ron was so turned off, he jetted out of there." –*Lauren, 32*

Careful with those hands!

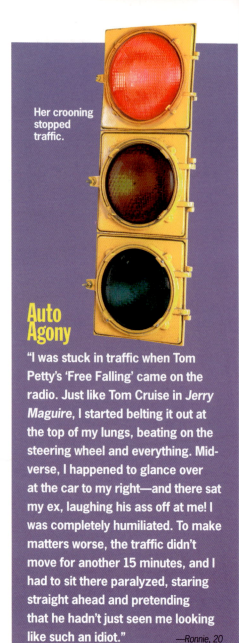

Her crooning stopped traffic.

Ex Marks the Spot

"I decided to take it easy one hungover Saturday night, so I was in full-on slob mode. I went to the video store for two movies and then picked up a super-value meal at a fast-food place. As I was walking home in my sweatpants, holding my videos in one hand and pulling french fries out of the bag with the other, I bumped into my high school boyfriend. He was dressed to kill—I knew even before he told me that he was headed out for a big date. We made conversation for a few minutes, then he leaned in to give me a hug good-bye. My french fry hand got caught against his chest, and when he pulled back, we both saw that I'd left a big ketchup splotch on his crisp white shirt. I felt like a complete geek, but thankfully, he was able to laugh it off." —Kimbra, 27

Auto Agony

"I was stuck in traffic when Tom Petty's 'Free Falling' came on the radio. Just like Tom Cruise in *Jerry Maguire*, I started belting it out at the top of my lungs, beating on the steering wheel and everything. Mid-verse, I happened to glance over at the car to my right—and there sat my ex, laughing his ass off at me! I was completely humiliated. To make matters worse, the traffic didn't move for another 15 minutes, and I had to sit there paralyzed, staring straight ahead and pretending that he hadn't just seen me looking like such an idiot." —Ronnie, 20

"I was walking home in sweats holding my videos and chowing on fries, when I bumped into my old boyfriend."

Shopping Showdown

"I'd dragged my new boyfriend shopping one Saturday. He sat in one of the chairs placed outside the dressing rooms while I went in and out, modeling various outfits for him. We were having a great time until I catwalked out to find my most recent ex sitting in the chair next to my new guy! To my horror, they were laughing and chatting with each other. I tried to run back into the dressing room to hide, but it was too late—they'd spotted me. I had no choice but to make the introductions. My boyfriend lost his grin and said, 'So this is the guy who was such a jerk to you?' They started yelling and I had to drag my guy into the dressing room with me, where I changed before we got the hell out of there!" —*Jana, 28*

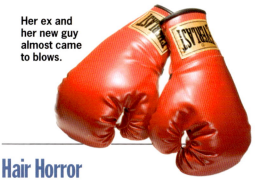

Her ex and her new guy almost came to blows.

Hair Horror

"My college swim team was going to Hawaii for training during our holiday break, so I decided to hit the tanning salon the week before. But I had no idea that the combo of the tanning lights and the chlorine was a recipe for disaster. Soon after I left the salon, I was out with a friend when my hair turned green! When she pointed it out, I hurried to the bathroom to check. On my way there, I ran into my ex, Doug. He immediately said, 'You look like the Grinch! Finally, your appearance matches your personality.' I wanted to smack him, but I was so self-conscious, I just ducked into the bathroom." —*Linda, 24*

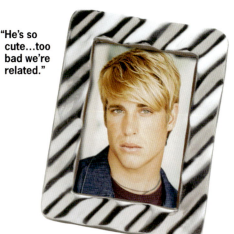

"He's so cute…too bad we're related."

Family Reunion

"A few weeks after my boyfriend Dave dumped me, my mother announced that she had invited my Lithuanian cousin, Kestutis, to visit. She kept telling me that showing him around would take my mind off things. I hadn't seen Kestutis since we were about 13 and when he stepped off the plane, I was surprised to see that he had blossomed into a total stud. Right then and there, I launched a campaign to make my ex jealous.

I knew this coffee shop where Dave went on weekends, so I took Kestutis there. When Dave walked in, I jumped onto poor unsuspecting Kestutis's lap and started playing with his hair and laughing. After a minute Dave walked over and said, 'I ran into your mom at the supermarket this morning and she told me you were entertaining your cousin from Lithuania today. I didn't know that meant you'd be giving him lap dances too.' I was so humiliated that I just walked out." —*Birute, 30*

13

THEIR LOSS!

Apparently, men are the ones who can't let go. According to a Public Opinion Strategies poll, 50 percent of single men still pine over an old flame compared to just 27 percent of single women.

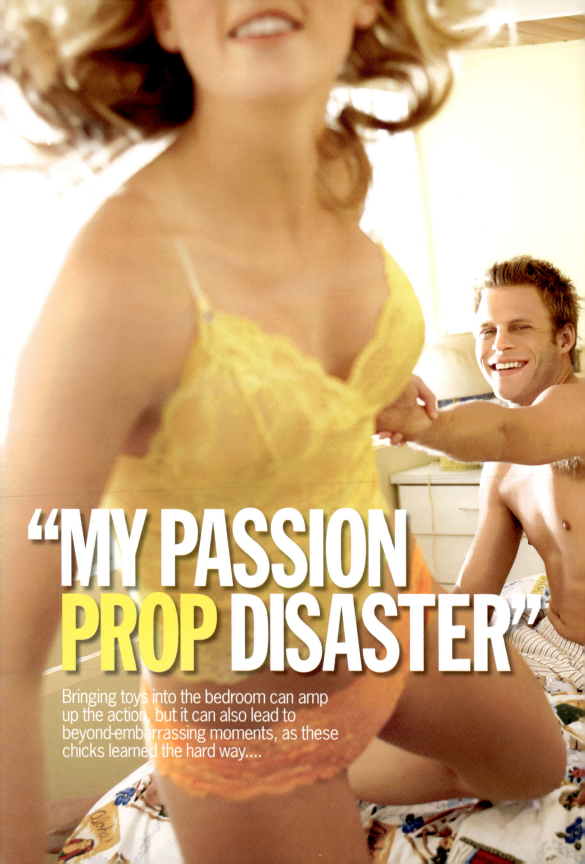

"MY PASSION
PROP DISASTER"

Bringing toys into the bedroom can amp
up the action, but it can also lead to
beyond-embarrassing moments, as these
chicks learned the hard way....

If you had a blunder like this girl, you'd bail too.

Cuff Her

"I had gotten pulled over for speeding on the freeway, and the cop asked for my license and registration. Just as I was reaching under the seat to grab my purse, though, he pulled out his gun and yelled 'Put your hands up and get out of the car!' Terrified, I did as I was told. Once he thought it was safe, he reached under the seat to find what he thought was a weapon, and instead pulled out the furry leopard-print handcuffs my boyfriend had given me as a joke. I'd stashed them there months ago and had forgotten about them. I was really embarrassed and had no idea what to say, so I just kept quiet. Thankfully, he started laughing and said that he'd let me go without giving me a ticket. There was one condition though: I'd have to let him keep the handcuffs. I quickly agreed, although I couldn't imagine who he was planning on arresting with those."　　—Paige, 32

14

Dolly Pardon

"My fiancé, Jake, has a 2-year-old nephew who found an inflatable sex doll that we'd received as a gag gift in our closet. I jokingly told the kid she was Jake's new girlfriend. A month or so later, we hosted an anniversary party for Jake's parents, and his sister commented on how nice it was to have the whole family together. Suddenly, his nephew said, 'Wait!' and ran down the hall. He came back to the living room with the doll and said, 'You forgot Uncle Jake's girlfriend.' I almost died!"　　—Lynne, 30

Office Space Case

"I work as an administrative assistant in a large office where everyone has their own little cubicle. One afternoon, my cell phone started ringing in my purse, and I scrambled to turn it off. I sit near several managers, and I didn't want them to think I was taking personal calls on company time. I couldn't find it right away, so I dumped the contents of my bag onto my desk and out came my

Listen up and she'll tell you what *not* to bring to work.

"I dumped the contents of my bag onto my desk and out came the last thing I wanted my boss to see."

vibrator, which I had brought to my guy's place the night before. Right as I grabbed it to stick it back in my bag, my boss approached my desk with a colleague and said, 'Hi, Kelly, I just wanted to introduce you to…oh, I see you're busy.' They abruptly turned and walked away as I stood there, frozen in shock, still holding the purple plastic toy in my hand."
—*Kelly, 32*

This pup can't distinguish between play toys.

Doggie-Style

"One afternoon, I was having some private time with my vibrator. I was almost finished when the doorbell rang, so I pulled on my robe and went to answer it. It was my boyfriend Roger and his parents, paying an impromptu visit. I invited them in and just as I excused myself to change, my dog Molly came running out of my room with my vibrator in her mouth. She dropped it right in front of Roger's dad, who patted Molly's head as he picked it up. I grabbed it from him, explaining it was a dog toy, but he gave me a look. I went back to my room, and when I came out, I overheard his mom say, 'I had no idea Kendra was so sex-crazed!'"
—*Kendra, 25*

DOUBLE DUTY FOR ALL YOUR NAUGHTY TOYS

Here are some semipractical uses for your amorous accoutrements:

Think that feather tickler looks like the perfect thing to dust your shelves with? It is!

Put that groovy-looking plastic member on your bookshelf and tell guests it's a sculpture you bought at a gallery for five grand.

Forget clothespins. Use those nipple clips to hang your fancy panties to dry.

Blender broken? Your high-powered vibrator will help you make your morning smoothie.

Quilt Trip

"One night my boyfriend Kevin came over with an array of goodies: lube, chocolate sauce, ropes—even a whip! The next morning we were running late, so I left, figuring I'd clean the bedroom after work. But when I pulled into the driveway that evening, I saw my aunt and uncle waiting on the porch. They had decided to drop in to say hi. When we all went inside, my aunt glanced into my bedroom and noticed the quilt she had made for me. I tried to run ahead of her, but it was too late. My aunt walked in, yelped, ran back to the living room, and rushed my uncle out the door as fast as she could. Later that evening, I got a call from my mother, who was sobbing about how she thought she'd raised me to be a decent young lady." —Erin, 24

Next time, remember to clean up your mess.

AN ORGASM A DAY...

A physician invented the vibrator in the 1880s to cure women with "hysteria"— a condition characterized by sexual fantasies, anxiety, and tension. Today, we just call it being horny.

SOURCE: THE TECHNOLOGY OF ORGASM: "HYSTERIA," THE VIBRATOR, AND WOMEN'S SEXUAL SATISFACTION BY RACHEL P. MAINES, PHD

OOPS! Baggage Buzz Kill

"I was flying home for Christmas vacation, and I packed my little vibrating friend. As I was going through airport security, the guard called me over to have my bags hand-checked. I had forgotten about my toy, and when he picked it up and asked what it was, I panicked and blurted, 'It's a back massager.' He grinned and held it up in the air so everyone around us could see, then he said, 'Oh, of course—my wife has one of these gadgets too.' I turned bright red, and as soon as he was done, I grabbed my bag and bolted." —Nina, 25

"Bzzzzzzzz zzzzzzzzzzzzzzzz zzzzzzzzzzzzzzzzzzzzz zzzzzzzzzzzzzzzz zzzzzzzzzz..."

14

X-Rated Exchange

"One Saturday afternoon, I needed to run a bunch of errands—one of which was to return a vibrator I'd received as a gag gift. I also had to exchange a leash I'd bought for my puppy. My first stop was the pet store, where I handed the manager the black plastic bag and told her I wanted something larger. When she looked in the bag, she got a strange look on her face and said she didn't think I purchased the item at their store. I started to argue, yelling something about the tag still being attached. Then, I reached in and pulled out the vibrator, right in front of a line of customers." —Anita, 36

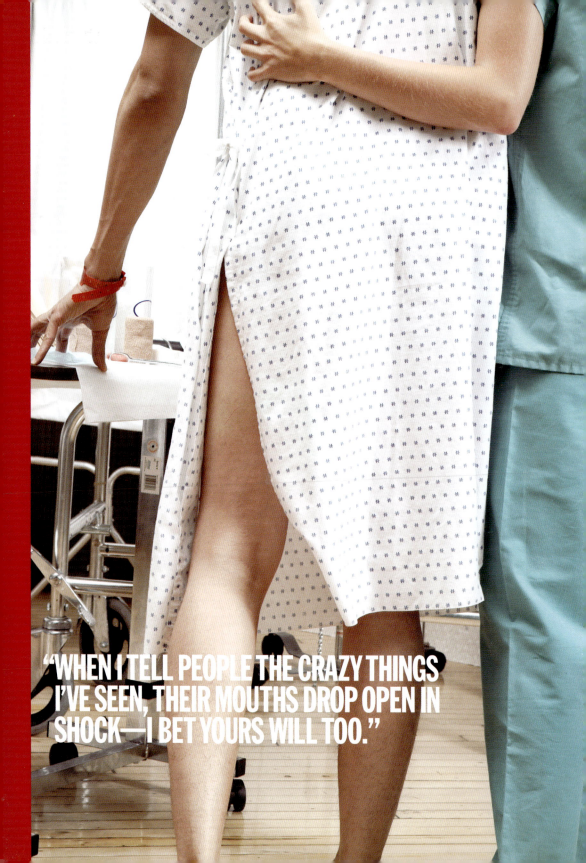

"WHEN I TELL PEOPLE THE CRAZY THINGS I'VE SEEN, THEIR MOUTHS DROP OPEN IN SHOCK—I BET YOURS WILL TOO."

CONFESSIONS OF
An ER Nurse

Freaky private parts, hilarious recovery-room come-ons, you name it and this poor woman has seen it on the job.

■ If you've ever spent any time in the hospital, whether it's in the OR or the ER, you've probably wondered just how closely the staff checks out the patients who come and go. As a nurse at a busy suburban hospital, I can tell you that we always remain as professional as possible… but we're still human. When we have an outrageous case, we definitely notice. And when I tell people some of the crazy things that go on behind the scenes, their mouths drop open in shock—I bet yours will too.

Naked Patients

My duties are pretty standard: I prep patients for surgery, wheel them to the OR, assist during operations, and attend to people in the recovery room as they are waking up from anesthesia. As you can tell, dealing with people's bodies is the basis of my job. Even though we try to keep patients covered, I wind up seeing nearly everyone naked at some point. I have to remove their hospital gowns when I'm putting in tubes or when I'm checking their incisions postsurgery. Although I'm used to seeing people in the buff, there are some things that catch my eye.

One time, I was prepping a patient for gallbladder surgery when he told me that he had to urinate, so I helped him use a plastic jug. When I lifted his gown, I almost fell over in shock—his unit was as thick as a soda can and hung halfway down to his knees! I kept my mouth shut and left him to do his business, but it was such an unbelievable sight that I had to show one of the other nurses. I didn't want to embarrass the patient, so I just asked my coworker to remove the urinal, telling her the patient was too sick to use his hands. She came back five minutes later with her face bright red! We agreed that it was a shame he couldn't donate half of his oversize organ to less genetically gifted men.

Another thing I see a lot of are penile implants—they are way more common than most people would think. Generally, they are used to cure chronic impotence. The implant is inserted into a soft penis, but it usually has a button the man can press through his skin to make the implant expand and become rigid to form an erection. Most of the time, the implants don't cause any problems—the men just warn me that they have an implant before I try

15

Confessions of an ER Nurse

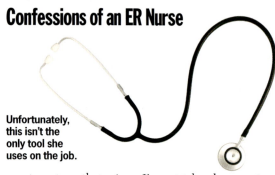

Unfortunately, this isn't the only tool she uses on the job.

to put a catheter in so I'm not taken by surprise. Hell, these guys often take great pleasure in showing me how well their apparatus works.

Bizarre Skin Art

I've also seen my share of weird tattoos. One woman came in for ob-gyn surgery, and I was taking care of her in the recovery room. The surgeon who'd just worked on her came in and told me to check her for bleeding, then added, "Don't go into Bob's house." I didn't know what he was talking about... until I saw that right above her privates was a tattoo that read "Bob's House" with an arrow pointing straight down! When I brought her back to her room after surgery, I met her boyfriend, Bob, and found out he was the artist who had inked her.

I also recently had a female patient who had her husband's name tattooed around her upper arm. Above the husband's name were four other wraparound tattoos in barbed-wire patterns, sort of like Pamela Anderson's. She told me that she had been married five times, and each time, she'd gotten her husband's name tattooed on her arm. After the

divorces, she couldn't stand the sight of those names, so she'd had them covered instead of removed because it was cheaper. She said that she'd never get another tattoo, but she'd consider another husband since men were easier to get rid of!

Peculiar Piercings

I have seen piercings on every body part imaginable. On women I see a lot of nipple piercings. Labia rings are becoming more common and so are penis rings. Most guys who have them just have a hoop threaded through their foreskin. But I saw one guy who had four! It seems to me like it would be painful, but every man I've asked says it increases his sexual pleasure. I have wondered what would happen if the hoop fell out during sex.

Tongue studs are also showing up a lot right now, especially with younger patients. But our anesthesiologists refuse to put someone under when they have a tongue stud in because, if it came loose, it could fall into the patient's lungs and cause major complications. I told one woman that rule and she refused to have the surgery! She swore that the hole closes up immediately after you remove the stud, which apparently is true. I guess, for some people, vanity is more important than their health.

Body-Cavity Mishaps

There is nothing worse than when I get called in for a foreign-body removal. That's a polite way of saying that somebody has stuck something inside himself and can't get it out. One of the strangest cases I've encountered happened to a man who had inserted a tiny rubber fishing lure into the hole at the end of his penis—the poor guy had read that it would help him last longer in bed! Well, somehow it got lost up there and we never got it out. The surgeon told him to come back if he had complications, but he never did.

One man came in with a vase stuck up his rear end! When we removed it, we discovered that it

ER LINGO

LOL	Little old lady
Bag 'Em	To put someone on a respirator
Facinoma	A fascinating ER story
Train Wreck	A patient with multiple problems

"Relax. This won't hurt a bit."

was at least 2 inches wide and 10 inches long! But here's the really bizarre part: A few weeks later, the same guy came back with another vase in his butt! We removed it and I wasn't going to give it back to him, but he begged, telling me it belonged to his mother. I let him have it, but only after making him swear that there wouldn't be a round three. Luckily, we have a piece of equipment called a grasper. The surgeon can put the patient to sleep, reach up, grab whatever's in there, and pull it back out.

Scandalous Sleep Talk

When the effects of anesthesia are wearing off, patients have lower inhibitions and say and do the most incredible things. They don't know how they act and they have no memory of anything later when they're fully conscious. I'm often the first person they see when they come to, so many of them spend their recovery time trying to grab me!

Recently, a guy I've known since high school came in for minor surgery, and I sat with him in the

> ## "WHEN THE ANESTHESIA IS JUST WEARING OFF, PATIENTS SAY THE MOST INCREDIBLE THINGS."

15

recovery room. He spent half an hour pleading with me to go on a date with him. By the time he was lucid enough to go back to his room—where his wife was waiting—he didn't remember a thing.

So like I said, I definitely see some wacky things in my line of work, but I wouldn't trade it for the world. I love helping others, and I develop a rapport with my patients. The doctors and nurses I work with are smart, talented people with great senses of humor. Thank God for that, because I'd go crazy if I didn't have someone to share this stuff with! ∎

FACT OR FICTION?

Can you guess which of these twisted hospital tales are true?

1 A woman in Louisiana came into the hospital to have a five-pound hair ball removed from her stomach. She admitted to having a lifelong habit of hair chewing.

2 A doctor in Massachusetts left a patient who was unconscious for a spinal-fusion procedure on the operating table for half an hour while he went to deposit a check.

3 A top Hollywood film producer refused to stay in the hospital after surgery unless all of her meals were delivered from five-star restaurants.

4 A 15-year-old hospital patient dialed an escort service from his room. When the prostitute showed up, the two got busy on the hospital bed.

NUMBERS 2 AND 4 ARE TRUE.

HYSTERICAL SEX SLIP-UPS

When you're desperate to get busy, bizarre things can happen, turning your carnal encounter into a circus act.

"We went back to his place, where he put the moves on me. I was ready... or so I thought!"

What a Gas!

"I'd been dating Stephen for just a few months, so I was still trying to maintain a good deal of mystery in our relationship. That meant no bodily functions in his vicinity at all. One night he took me out for Indian food, which really doesn't agree with me. I just wanted to go home afterward, but he begged me to come over and watch a movie. I figured it would be no big deal as long as we didn't hook up. Well, after a couple of hours, I was feeling a bit better, so when he put the moves on I was ready...or so I thought. In the middle of doing the deed, I let one rip! (And let's just say that I was in a less than flattering position.) Mortified, I immediately jumped off the bed just as my guy laughed and said, 'Damn girl, what did you eat?' In a split second I had killed the mystery." —*Kelly, 30*

16

Name Flopper

"Even though I was in love with my girlfriend, I had been dipping my wick elsewhere. One night, we went out, and I tossed back a few beers and was feeling really good. My girlfriend ended up taking me home early. We fell into bed and started fooling around. When things got hot and heavy I whispered in her ear, 'It's okay, as long as Lisa doesn't find out.' The problem with this statement: My girlfriend *is* Lisa! In my idiotic stupor I thought I was cheating on my girlfriend instead of having sex with her! She dumped me first thing the next morning." —*Josh, 29*

He loved her for her locks.

Cold Turkey

"I was staying at my parents' house for Thanksgiving, and one night while my folks were asleep, I grabbed a magazine and took it with me into the bathroom. Desperate for visual stimulation, I taped a photo of the *Seinfeld* cast to the shower wall so I could stare at Elaine. In the morning I found the picture stuck to the bathroom mirror with a note from my mom that said we needed to talk. She ended up accusing me of being gay. 'You were showering with Jerry, George, and Kramer!' she yelled."

—Jeff, 28

These two took the randy road less traveled.

Wigged Out

"I went out with this girl who had gorgeous long brown hair. I took her to dinner and things went really well, so we wound up going back to my place. I lit some candles to set the mood, and we started kissing. When I slipped my fingers through her ponytail, though, it came loose, landed on one of the candles, and caught ablaze! She screamed, threw the hair on the floor, and stamped it out. After she calmed down, she told me she'd gotten a terrible haircut that morning so she'd bought extensions for our night out. I thought it was kind of gross, so I made up a lame excuse about having to go to work early the next day and ended the date."

—Keith, 20

"I lit some candles, then ran my fingers through her ponytail, which came loose...."

Romp and Roll

"My girlfriend and I decided to have a make-out session like we did back in high school, so we drove up to a lookout point, popped a '90s CD into the stereo, and stretched out on the floor of my flatbed. Our heavy petting escalated, and in no time, we were really 'rocking the casbah.' Just as I was about to orgasm, I felt a jolt, which I assumed was my girlfriend. But when the truck really started bouncing, we realized we were rolling down the hill! There was no time to grab our clothes, so we jumped out and landed in a pile of leaves. We watched the truck roll on for a few yards before it dropped off the edge of the hillside. The relief we felt about escaping unscathed was short-lived when we realized we would have to make our way back to civilization—naked." —Charlie, 31

"In the middle of the night, I woke up to hear my girl screaming like crazy...."

This chick's choppers really failed her.

Wet and Vile

"Monica and I had been out three times, and it was clear that the fourth date would be 'the night.' We went to dinner and shared a bottle of wine. Then we hung out at a friend's party, where we drank some more. Even though I was a bit woozy, I still wanted to sleep with Monica. But she insisted that our first time be special, not sloppy. I swore up and down that I was sober, and she believed me. We ended up having great—albeit clumsy—sex. Everything would have been great, except that in the middle of the night, I woke up to hear Monica screaming like crazy. I opened my eyes and realized that in my sleep I had accidentally wet the bed! She was so disgusted, she kicked me out of her apartment and told me never to call her again."

—Michael, 25

Jaws, the Sequel

"In my first semester of college a group of my guy friends and I threw a wild party. This cute girl, Carol, who commuted from home and usually didn't go to parties, showed. We chatted, and after a while, I invited her up to my room. We began making out and got naked. Eventually Carol decided to give me a little below-the-belt action, but in the middle of doing her thing, she pulled away. She turned on the light, and I noticed her mouth was wide open. She started talking, but I couldn't understand a word she was saying.

"Her mouth was wide open and she was talking, but I couldn't understand a word she was saying."

Finally she grabbed a piece of paper and wrote 'lock jaw, mouth stuck.' I later found out she has a medical condition in which her facial muscles spasm and her jaw becomes locked in place if she leaves her mouth open for too long. I asked her if there was anyone I could contact, and she scrawled 'Mom.' Carol wrote down the number, and I had to make the call. Her mother insisted on picking Carol up, so I threw on some clothes and Carol got dressed too. When her mom arrived at my apartment to retrieve her, I couldn't make eye contact."

—Robbie, 19

16

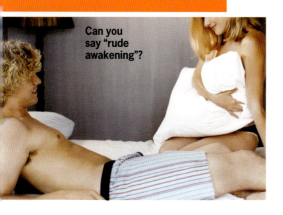

Can you say "rude awakening"?

He's not the only one who went rolling in the mud.

Roadside Ass-istance

"My boyfriend Brett was moving, and at his going-away party we wanted to get it on one last time. Luckily, the host ran out of ice, so Brett and I had an excuse to leave for a quickie. It was raining, and the only way we could get to the store was on Brett's four-wheeler. Halfway down the road we pulled into a ditch and had crazy sex in the pouring rain. When we went to put our clothes back on, though, we realized they had fallen off the ATV and were completely drenched in mud. By the time we got back to the party, we were so filthy that we had to tell everyone we'd flipped the four-wheeler." —Samantha, 20

Sex-Tional Sofa

"My boyfriend and I were staying at my grammy's place, which is small, so we slept on this old, ratty couch in the den. Since my grandmother is deaf and was sleeping upstairs, my boyfriend and I decided to get a little frisky. Just as things started getting really good, we heard a crack, and the sofa split in two, sending us crashing to the floor. The next morning we tried to make excuses for the disaster to my grandmother, but she just laughed and said, 'You can't fool me, kids. Whaddya think Gramps and I did on that couch for 35 years?'" —Katie, 25

Pity in Pink

SMOOTH MOVE

"I have a lot of female friends who come to me as a shoulder to cry on. A few weeks ago my friend Melanie showed up at my place, upset because she'd had a fight with her roommate. I poured us some wine, and we talked for a while. Then out of nowhere, she kissed me. Melanie is really cute, so I was all for it, and pretty soon things were getting very steamy. Just as we were about to take our clothes off, I remembered that I was wearing pink bikini underwear, a gag gift from an old girlfriend and, unfortunately, the only clean Skivvies I had around. When Melanie started undoing my pants, I grabbed my wine as though I was going to take a sip and spilled it all over my lap. I kept saying, 'Oh man, I am such an idiot!' and then ran to the bathroom to take off the pants and the girlie underwear. When I came back out completely naked, my little accident was immediately forgotten and we got down to business." —Carl, 22

From now on, he'll remember laundry day.

If I'd known we'd be taping, I'd have worn my red panty set.

Girl on Film

"One night my boyfriend and I were feeling naughty, so we decided to take pictures of ourselves in the act. The pics turned out pretty good, and I downloaded them to my computer so I could create an album for my man. But the next morning I got a better

The pics turned out pretty good, and I downloaded them to my computer so I could create an album for my man.

idea: I wrote up a racy e-mail, inviting my guy to join me for a repeat performance and attached the pics from the night before. Well, when he came over that night, he said he'd never gotten them. I checked my out-box and realized that I'd accidentally sent the e-mail and pictures to my uncle!" —Jill, 32

First their passion soared, then it took a nosedive.

Rooftop Party

"Last New Year's Eve my girlfriend and I went to a friend's house party and decided to fool around on the roof. We climbed out the attic window and started going at it. Suddenly I looked up and saw a face in the window. Startled, I jumped up and fell backward—off the roof. I landed in the bushes one floor down and broke my arm. The pain was bad, but the worst part was lying there, pants around my ankles, with my package hanging out." —Sam, 27

16

22% OF WOMEN HAVE TAKEN NAUGHTY PICS AND HAD THEM DISCOVERED.

"The Usual" Suspect

"I met my boyfriend Kyle on vacation, and we fell so in love that we decided to try a long-distance relationship. Although I cared about Kyle, I still had needs, and I was having casual encounters with random guys here and there. Whenever I needed condoms, I'd run into the convenience store around the corner. Since I usually go at about the same time (late at night, on my way home), the guy behind the counter knows me and hands me the condoms and an orange juice without my even having to ask. When Kyle finally came to visit, the two of us stopped at the convenience store on the way home so he could get a soda. As soon as the convenience store guy saw me, he grabbed my brand of condoms, threw them on the counter, and with a smile said, 'Your usual.'" —Alison, 32

"The guy at the store knows me and hands me my 'usual' without my having to ask."

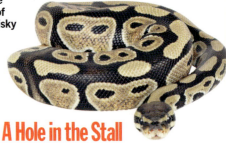

One of the dangers of getting frisky alfresco

A Hole in the Stall

"My girlfriend and I were at an outdoor concert and were really enjoying ourselves. I don't know if it was the heat or the skimpy outfits, but we started feeling frisky. Problem was, we couldn't find a private area. We finally decided to get it on in the grossest place ever…the port-a-potty! After finding a relatively clean one that didn't smell too nasty, we started going at it. Halfway through, I looked down and saw a small snake that seemed to have wiggled through a hole in the stall. I happen to be terrified of snakes, so my fear kicked in, and I freaked out. I bolted out of the port-a-potty with my pants around my ankles, leaving the door wide open and my girlfriend exposed for all to see." —Paul, 21

HOW TO... RECOVER FROM A SEX SLIP

Save face after an embarrassing mattress moment and set the mood again.

Laugh It Off Rather than hiding under the covers, try to make light of your bedroom blunder by throwing out a one-liner like, "Wow, the earth must have moved because I fell right out of bed," or whatever fits the situation. Joking about it will make it seem like less of a big deal.

Flatter Him Boosting your man's ego is a good way to deflect an awkward moment and get back on track. So you passed gas in bed? Try saying something like, "You had me so caught up in the moment that I couldn't control myself." He'll want to get back to rocking your world ASAP.

Chill Out Sometimes, no matter how hard you try, the magic of the moment is gone. Instead of forcing things, just kick back—cuddle or engage in some intimate pillow talk. Before long, your lust levels may start heating up again. SOURCE: YVONNE K. FULBRIGHT, SEXOLOGIST AND AUTHOR OF *THE HOT GUIDE TO SAFER SEX*

Kissing Cousins

"My girlfriend Cathy and I were at a house party when I ran into an ex, Laurie. Cathy had never met Laurie, and when she saw me chatting with her, she got jealous and pulled me away. To calm her down, I told her that Laurie was my cousin. Toward the end of the night, Laurie cornered me. She led me into one of the bedrooms, where we were going at it until Cathy stormed in. She totally lost it and ran out. Then she yelled in front of everyone, 'I can't believe you're sick enough to have sex with your cousin!'" —Hank, 26

Maybe he should have used this to cover his butt.

Spicy Dish

"After seeing a photo spread of 'Naked Chefs' in an issue of *Cosmo*, I decided to buy my boyfriend an apron. He laughed and promised to cook for my birthday. The following night I was out with my dad, and I invited him back to my apartment. As we were coming up the stairs, I could smell onions cooking and realized my beau was making dinner. It didn't occur to me that he would be doing it bare assed! You can imagine my father's shock when he saw my guy in nothing but an apron." —Sarah, 25

"It looks like someone needs a trim."

Bushwhacking Blunder

"My girlfriend and I have been together for years, so most of the mystery is gone. For the past five months she's been asking me to trim her pubic hair for her, so I decided to give in. One afternoon my girlfriend called me into the bathroom, where I found her standing over the toilet, beard trimmer in hand for me. She held on to the counter and leaned back while I tried to figure out how the thing worked. After going at it for a bit I realized I'd done something wrong. She was totally bald down there! I gasped and said, 'Honey, I think I messed up!' She freaked out, yanked the contraption out of my hand, and told me I was never allowed near her with the trimmer again." —James, 24

16

"One afternoon, my girlfriend called me into the bathroom, where she made a request."

For one couple, this lube spelled trouble.

Hot Pocket

"My girlfriend and I were staying at her parents' house for a week. One night we were feeling a little kinky and visited a sex shop together. On the way out, we bought some heat-activated lube, which I put in my pocket. When we got back to her house, I couldn't find my wallet, so I frantically pulled

"While I was hunting for my wallet, my girlfriend's dad called my name and asked, 'Um, is this yours?'"

everything out of my pockets and left it all on the kitchen table. While I was hunting for my wallet in the living room, I heard my girlfriend's dad call my name and ask, 'Um, is this yours?' Thinking he meant my wallet, I eagerly ran over and told him I was sure it was. Much to my dismay, I noticed he was cluelessly holding the container of lube! He has really bad eyesight, so he put on his glasses and began reading the front of the package. When he realized what it was, he freaked out and insisted my girlfriend and I sleep in separate rooms for the rest of the week."

—Alex, 30

Untasty Treat

"My man had a rough day, so I decided to make him feel better. I was kissing my way down his stomach when I got this horrible taste in my mouth. I began to gag, so I ran into the bathroom to wash out my mouth with water. Meanwhile, my boyfriend grabbed his shirt to see what might have been on it. It smelled funny, so he checked the dresser and realized he'd used carpet cleaner on his shirt instead of static spray." *—Suzanne, 30*

Flop-Up Video

"Dan and I had been dating for six months when he confessed that he had a fantasy about watching me pleasure myself. I felt too self-conscious to give him a live performance, but I came up with the idea of videotaping myself in action for him. When I showed him the tape, he was totally turned on, until it cut to my parents waving into the camera at my niece's fifth birthday party, then switched back to me doing my thing before it cut back to my niece. It was so creepy and weird that we hit eject and tossed the tape." *—Pamela, 27*

Some moments are destined to wind up on the cutting-room floor.

> **"Things were getting really wild when all of a sudden we heard a loud crack."**

Trailer Trashed OOPS!

"I met this hot girl, Megan, at a club one night, and we totally hit it off. I don't bring girls home with me very often because I live with my mom in a trailer. They're usually not very impressed by that, but this girl was so sweet and irresistible, I brought her back to my place, and before long, we were in my bed. She was on top, and things were getting really wild when I heard a loud crack. The next thing I knew, the foot of the bed fell through the floor of the mobile home, and we were suddenly having sex at a 45-degree angle! I didn't get to enjoy it, though, because Megan jumped off me and left as fast as she could. When my mom came home and found a huge hole in the floor, I had some explaining to do."

—Rick, 21

Erotic Ex-Clamation

"I was on a date with this great guy, Kevin, when we started discussing our families. My twin brother, Tom, and I are really close, so I talked a lot about him. Unfortunately, I had neglected to mention that my recent ex was also named Tom. Later, we went back to Kevin's place to hook up. As I was hitting my peak, I mistakenly cried out, 'Oh, Tom! Oh, Tom!' Kevin immediately stopped what he was doing and looked at me like I was a pervert. He called me a sicko and kicked me out of his house without even waiting to hear my excuse."

—Sandra, 24

16

20% OF WOMEN HAVE SHOUTED OUT THE WRONG NAME IN BED.

"Let's get busy before something else goes wrong."

Breaking and Entering

"One night when we were sharing our secret desires, my girlfriend told me she'd always had a fantasy of breaking into a stranger's house to have sex. A few weeks later I saw my chance to show her the next best thing when my parents' friends asked me to house-sit. Without letting on that I knew the owners, I drove my girlfriend to the house, and we crept in through a window. We were having mind-blowing sex in the living room when in walked the next-door neighbor with a baseball bat! He'd seen us climb in through the window and figured we were burglars." —*Ed, 26*

"Without letting on that I knew the owners, we drove to the house and crept in the window."

Aww, poor pussycat!

Cat's Me-Ewww

"One night I met a great girl at a club, and we started making out. I invited her back to my place even though the apartment was a total mess. I threw the comforter over my unmade bed, and we jumped on top and started going at it. Things got so hot that we slipped under the covers to really get the party started. After a few minutes we both realized we were squishing around in something. We climbed out of bed and discovered that my cat had gotten sick all over the sheets. The hottie and I both ran to the shower to wash ourselves off. Unfortunately, neither of us was really in the mood for sex after that." —*James, 23*

Sticky Situation

"My girlfriend heard that toothpaste would enhance oral sex. That night she bought a tube and tried it by squirting a bunch in her mouth and going down on me. Everything was fine—until her mouth got sticky. When she started to gag, I realized we had a problem. I helped pry her mouth away from me, and we rushed into the bathroom for a good rinse. We discovered she hadn't used toothpaste but denture adhesive!" —Chris, 23

This girl should brush up on her sex tricks.

Full-Service Dining

"On our first anniversary, my girlfriend and I went to dinner at a cozy, romantic restaurant. Halfway through the meal, Holly accidentally dropped her napkin. When she bent down to pick it up, she got a very naughty idea. The place was dimly lit, so she slipped under the table, unzipped my pants, and started going to work on me. I was enjoying it until I saw my aunt and uncle—who coincidentally were eating at the same restaurant—approaching the table. Apparently, the thrill of getting caught got Holly more excited because she worked even harder at pleasing me. I ended up finishing with my aunt and uncle standing right over me!" —Seth, 23

Relax. There's no cause for alarm.

Trigger Happy

"The summer before we left for college my girlfriend and I spent a lot of time hooking up in her parents' basement while they were asleep upstairs. One night we were making out with our clothes on. Suddenly her father came running downstairs in his bright red bathrobe and slippers, so we stopped kissing immediately. I thought I was in the clear until I saw that he was carrying a 12-gauge shotgun! I panicked and moved as far away from my girlfriend as possible. I was terrified that her dad was planning to shoot me right then and there, but he sprinted

"I was terrified that her dad was planning to shoot me, but he sprinted past us and went out the door."

past us and went out the door. It turned out that hordes of raccoons were destroying their prized family garden, and her father was staging a surprise attack. Even though he wasn't going after me, the image of my girlfriend's burly father with a shotgun ruined the mood that night. From then on I insisted we get it on in the car or at my place instead." —Frank, 20

16

"EW! I CAN'T BELIEVE I HOOKED UP WITH HIM"

Check out these horrifying but hysterical stories from women who went to bed with a stud and woke up with a dud. Warning: After reading this, you may want to inspect the next guy you meet under a floodlight.

"But you looked so sexy last night in the dark."

Gummy Scare

"My coworker was having a housewarming party, and I was dreading it. But 30 minutes into it, this guy came up to me who was sweet and cute. After hanging out for a while, he asked if I wanted to go back to his place 'just to talk.' I agreed, and we ended up fooling around before drifting off to sleep. At 9 a.m., I rolled over, excited for another round with this guy. But when he smiled, I saw that he was missing his front teeth! With a big stupid grin, he said, 'I take my teeth out at night. See?' and pointed to the nightstand where his dentures were soaking in a glass. He seemed to think it was hysterical, but I was so grossed out that I got out of there as quickly as I could. The poor guy kept calling, but I wouldn't answer the phone!"   —Carla, 24

Senior Sinner

"One night my pals and I hit the town on a mission to meet men. The club we picked kind of sucked, so we decided to go to a local bar instead. It was dimly lit in there, but I spotted this rugged-looking man with a shaved head across the room. We made eyes at each other until I finally got up the nerve to go over and talk to him. At the end of the night, after a few martinis, he asked if I wanted to go back to his house and use his hot tub. I agreed. After enjoying the best sex of my life, I woke up smiling. But when I looked at the man next to me, I almost cried. The guy was about 55 years old, with wrinkles and age spots. I made up an excuse and took off. It's too bad, though, because, clearly, older men are skilled in the sack."   —Rita, 27

17

She should have guessed his age when she saw those sneakers.

If a guy pulls out one of these, run!

Kiss and Makeup

"At a club one night, this hottie came up and started talking to me. I invited him home, and we had a lot of fun. When he woke me up the following day, I saw that he had been wearing mascara, which was now streaked under his eyes. Apparently, he'd also been sporting cream foundation, because it rubbed off on my white pillowcases. I asked if he was a drag queen and he said, 'No, not at all. I just think it makes me look better.' I've heard of metrosexuals, but this was too much." —Katie, 30

Teeny Bop-per

"I was at a frat party with some friends when I met Craig. He was one of the hottest guys I'd ever seen, so I agreed to go back to his place. When we walked into his house, he insisted that I be very quiet, which I thought was a little odd. We went into his room and had the most incredible sex for hours. The next morning, I woke up to the smell of bacon frying. I whispered, 'Is your housemate making breakfast?' to which he responded, 'Housemate? That's my mom. I'm still in high school.' The man of my dreams was only 16! The worst part was we had to sit and have breakfast with his parents and little sister." —Emily, 20

"When we walked into his house, he insisted I be quiet, which was odd...."

HOW TO... GET RID OF HIM

Here are three ways to kick last night's mistake out the door.

Lie a Little Make up an excuse about something you have to do that morning like, "Sorry, but my parents are coming over any minute to take me out to brunch. That way he'll leave without any why-don't-you-like-me drama.

Get His Digits Asking for his number (even if you don't intend to call) is a way to say goodbye without killing his confidence. If he wants yours in return, explain that you're always busy, so it'll be easier for you to ring him.

Play the Casual Card Let him down gently by saying that you're not looking for a long-term thing: "This was fun, but I just got out of a relationship, and I'm not ready to date."

SOURCE: MICHAEL CUNNINGHAM, PHD, PSYCHOLOGIST, UNIVERSITY OF LOUISVILLE

Friend in Need

"One New Year's Eve I met this guy who was good-looking and hilarious. We hung out most of the night, and since we had a friend in common, I decided it was safe to invite him over. We kissed and made out for a while before falling asleep. I woke up a few hours later to him snuggling against me, which I thought was really sweet...until I realized he was sobbing. I asked what was wrong and he blubbered, 'Don't make me go home. My fiancée broke up with me on our wedding day a month ago and I don't want to be alone.' I wish my friend had told me that before letting me bring this dude home!" —Marla, 32

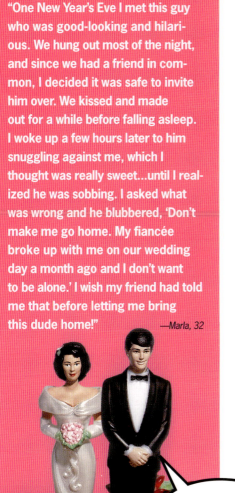

"Puhlease, stay with me forever and ever!"

Every awkward situation should come with an easy exit.

Big Daddy

"I met this seriously sexy stranger at a bar, and we flirted all night. When last call came, he invited me back to his place. Even though I'd never done that sort of thing before, I gave in to my lustful feelings and agreed. When we woke up the next day, he looked at me and said, 'Next time we do this, you can be the daddy.' I was out of there in no time!" —Laura, 29

"I didn't regret what I'd done, until I found out about his bizarre hobby...."

Gimme an O...No!

"When I was in college, I was introduced to this cute guy at a homecoming party, and I slept with him. He was lots of fun in bed, and we had a great time, so I did not regret it until the next morning. We were lying there when he said, 'You know, it's so refreshing to meet a girl who's open-minded enough to accept the fact that I'm a cheerleader.' I don't know how I'd missed that bizarre detail during our get-to-know-you conversation, but when he busted out a cheerleading move on his way to the bathroom, I knew I had to leave. After that, I vowed never to hook up on the first date again." —Holly, 23

17

67%
OF READERS HAVE BEEN GROSSED OUT THE MORNING AFTER A HOOKUP.

"I'M GOING TO GIVE YOU THE LOWDOWN ON EVERYTHING, INCLUDING THE SINFUL STORIES OUR CLIENTS TELL US, THE RIDICULOUS DEMANDS PEOPLE MAKE, AND MORE...."

CONFESSIONS OF

A Masseuse

A massage therapist reveals the dirty details of her job, from come-ons to gross-outs. Plus, the shocking secret she told only *Cosmo*.

■ Chances are, if you're in your 20s, you've indulged in a professional full-body massage. But as sumptuous as it might be, you've probably also wondered what your massager is thinking as he or she kneads your bare body. Is she checking out my cellulite? Does touching me turn him on?

Well, you're about to find out. I'm going to give you the lowdown on what goes through masseuses' minds, including what we think about during a massage, the sinful stories our clients tell us, the outrageous demands people make, and more. Plus, I'll let you in on an X-rated secret that I've never told anyone.

Handling Hot Hunks

I love doing massage. Hokey as it sounds, I like making people feel good. But there's another perk: I get to ogle delicious eye candy. When a gorgeous guy with a smooth back and heavenly muscle tone comes in, I definitely fantasize. But as tempting as it might be, I don't get physical with my customers because that could cost me my license. That's not to say I've never done anything with a *former* client, though.

Three years ago, a man with a spectacular physique walked into my studio. I loved kneading his body, and when he started coming in regularly, I couldn't wait to get my hands on him. The sexual energy between us became so intense that every time I touched him, I felt like an electrical current was running through me.

Finally, I couldn't take the frustration of massaging him, daydreaming about him, and not being able to go any further. So after a few months, I confessed my feelings to him. I was so bummed as I said the words, "I can't see you as a client anymore." But when he said, "Well, let's get some dinner then," my knees practically gave out. We had a passionate affair for five exciting months. Once the sexual heat started to fade, we split up, but I wouldn't trade that lusty experience for anything in the world.

18

"HALFWAY THROUGH THE MASSAGE, THE OLD GUY GRINNED AND SAID, 'OH, LOOK HOW HOT YOU'RE MAKING ME.' I WAS SO DISGUSTED THAT I JUST RAN OUT OF THERE...."

Quirky Clients

On the other hand, I've had my share of male customers who were so lewd, they made me want to run screaming from the room. This happened on my first masseuse job at an athletic club. My client was a normal-looking, middle-aged man. But halfway through the massage, he pointed to his penis beneath the towel and said, "Oh, look how hot you're making me." I was so disgusted, I spun on my heels and ran out of there, even though my teachers had warned me that this kind of thing would happen.

I've gotten used to the spontaneous erections, though. It's natural for a guy to get hard while being worked on. I pretend not to notice, and usually the guy is decent enough to let the "situation" pass without saying anything.

Despite the occasional pervert, I've developed some close professional relationships with my male clients. Most of them are in their 40s and 50s, with high-paying, high-stress jobs. They come to me for relief from the pressures of their daily lives, and a lot of them just lie on the table and spill their guts.

A few years ago, a married man who'd been seeing me regularly started telling me about his illicit love affair every time he came in. Clearly, this guy just needed someone to talk to. As he rambled on about how much he loved his wife and his mistress, though, I thought, *Why on earth are you telling me this? I'm not a psychiatrist!* But sometimes I think I might as well be.

I see plenty of women too. The single chicks come in and tell me all the sordid details of their wild parties and sexual adventures. But I have a hard time relating to the "ladies who lunch," you know, those rich middle-aged women who have nothing to do all day. They flop down on

RUB FLUBS
Readers fess up to their most mortifying massage-table experiences.

"I went to a spa with a friend, and we got massages together. After my rubdown, my male masseuse mumbled something to my friend's masseuse. She came over to me and whispered, 'You should change your tampon.' I'd forgotten and had an overspill."
—Kelly, 25

"A masseuse mentioned that she could see through my underwear that I was a natural redhead. Talk about making someone uncomfortable! I never went back there again."
—Suzanne, 22

"I was getting an amazing massage at a very swanky spa when I opened my eyes and noticed that my masseuse, who was wearing drawstring pants, had a massive erection! I couldn't relax after that, and it ruined the experience for me."
—Gillian, 2

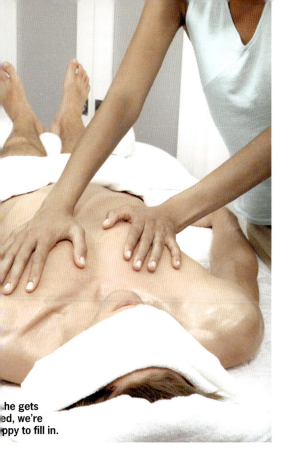

he gets
ed, we're
ppy to fill in.

Comfort in Colleagues

The oddities of this profession foster close friendships among coworkers. We'll go out after work, sip cocktails, and dish. We're there for one another when we need to vent. We also have fun blowing off steam by imitating demanding clients and swapping stories about on-the-job gross-outs like "back-ne" (pimply backs).

Many of my customers are obese, and sometimes I look at them and all I can think is, *God, how can she let herself get like this?* But the real problem I have with some customers is their smell. Perspiration gets caught between folds of flesh, causing bad body odor. You'd think some people would shower and scrub more.

Although I've been doing massage for five years, there are some things I will never get used to and some things I wish I could forget. I play by the rules now, but things were different before I got my license.

A Secret Revealed

When I moved to New York City six years ago, I had dreams of becoming an actress. But when I realized that I was never going to see my name in lights on Broadway, I decided to become a professional masseuse because I

the table like they're carrying the weight of the world on their shoulders. They complain about how miserable their lives are and say the nastiest things about their friends behind their backs. It's seriously *so* boring. Most of the time, I just tune them out and start going over my to-do list or planning my next vacation.

"I stopped in at one of those small nail salons that also do massage. My masseuse was an old man who could hardly hear. Whenever I said 'softer,' he'd just work me harder. t was awful!" —Tara, 33

"I went to a spa that had me fill out a form beforehand. Where they asked me to list my allergies, I wrote that I had a reaction to mango. I guess no one read my form because they massaged me with mango oil, and I got a horrible rash." —Melissa, 28

"I was skiing and stopped in at the lodge spa for a full-body rub. It was so good, in fact, that halfway through it, I started sobbing hysterically, and my hot masseuse had to bring me some tissues." —Sierra, 30

18

Confessions of a Masseuse

heard you could make great money. I started taking classes to get my license and bartended at night to support myself. But having to work until 4:30 in the morning turned me into a total zombie at school. It was a struggle.

One day, after a particularly exhausting week juggling the bar and classes, I was perusing the want ads and came across one calling for sensual masseuses. I remembered a girl I'd met a while ago who told me that she made amazing money doing relief massage. (It entailed working at a massage parlor, where you

come close to being promiscuous. But if I could pull in $180 for each relief massage, I rationalized I could get over my reservations.

When I went to work that first day, my legs were shaking as I was led to the massage room. There, on his stomach, lay a naked flabby man in his 50s. I felt repulsed just touching him. And when I finished him off, I thought I would vomit. As soon as he left, I scrubbed my hands raw with soap and the hottest water I could stand.

Doing relief massages gradually got a little easier. Most of the guys were professional

"GUYS I DATE OFTEN EXPECT ME TO GIVE THEM MASSAGES, BUT THE LAST THING I WANT TO DO WHEN I GET HOME IS MORE WORK!"

get naked, give a guy a massage, and then finish by manually stimulating him.)

When I told her about the ad, she suggested that I look into it. My immediate reaction was, "Are you kidding? No way!" It sounded not only dirty, but illegal. Still, I had become passionate about getting my massage license and I wasn't going to let tuition money stand in my way. So without letting myself think about it too much, I set up an appointment to meet the salon owner the next day.

She told me I didn't need any formal massage experience, but asked, "I assume you know how to please a guy below the belt with your hands?" I emphatically responded "Yes!" even though my mind was screaming *No!* The night before I saw my first client, I felt sick. I was thinking, *What the hell am I doing?* I had never even

married men who just wanted to blow off a little steam—not so unlike those who come to me now. And concentrating on getting my massage license helped me get through it. Once I finished school and got a legitimate job, I took a massive pay cut. But it was worth it: I'd much rather earn my living in an honest way than doing what I'd been doing.

These days, the guys I date often expect me to give them massages, but the last thing I want to do when I get home at the end of a long day is more work! (If you were an accountant, would you want to do your boyfriend's bills after putting in a full day at the office?) On the other hand, when a guy wants to rub *me* with oil and give *me* a massage, I'm a very happy and willing recipient—although I may have to give him a few pointers. ∎

MASSAGE ON THE RISE

According to the American Massage Therapy Association, 21% of adults had a massage in 2004, compared to just 8% in 1997.

8% 1997

21% 2004

CAUGHT WITH THEIR PANTIES DOWN

These randy readers set out to have a red-hot sex session, but when they were busted mid-booty, they wound up red in the face instead.

ANNA PALMA

She didn't really need those undies anyway.

Secrets and Lice

"My fiancé and I were staying at my parents' place for the weekend, and on our last night, they took us out for an expensive meal. We had a bottle of wine and the oyster appetizer, so on the ride home, we had a hard time keeping our hands off each other. After everyone went to bed, my guy and I started hooking up in the den. I had just taken off all of his clothes and he was starting to strip me down when my 15-year-old brother walked into the room and turned on the light. I freaked and blurted the first thing that popped into my head: 'I had to check his body for lice!' My brother just told me he wasn't stupid, then turned off the light and walked out." —*Alexandra, 28*

Who's Your Daddy?

"I brought my hot new hunk to my parents' country house for the weekend. When we arrived, the place was totally empty, so we raced upstairs to my childhood bedroom for a little pre-parental-meeting passion. I don't know if it was the pink canopy bed or the rows of stuffed animals, but my guy was totally geting into the fantasy. He began whispering kinky things in my ear like, 'Are you Daddy's girl? Do you love your daddy?' I was getting really turned on and started screaming 'Oh yes, Daddy!' Suddenly there was a knock at the door. 'Sweetheart?' my actual dad said in an alarmed voice. 'Is everything okay in there?' Apparently, they'd decided to drive up, and we were too involved in what we were doing to hear them arrive. We didn't even bother explaining and just came downstairs 10 minutes later for the most uncomfortable family dinner ever! None of us could even look at anyone else." —*Sally, 24*

19

Man, that vista is such a turn-on.

Early Riser

"I was on vacation with my boyfriend Omar and my parents in Hawaii and was really looking forward to some R&R. Unfortunately, though, my parents had gotten us adjoining rooms because they thought it would be 'more fun.' Omar and I realized that if we were going to get it on, it would have to be early, while my folks were still

"My parents got us all adjoining rooms, thinking it would be more fun."

asleep. So on the first night, we set the alarm for 5 a.m. so we could be sure to squeeze in some action before they woke up. The second it went off, we got down to business. Well, we had no idea how thin the walls were because the alarm also woke my dad, who walked into our room (without knocking) to ask why we were up before dawn. He got his answer when he saw Omar on top of me!" —Melanie, 34

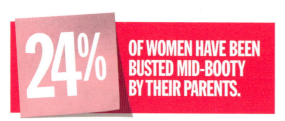

24% OF WOMEN HAVE BEEN BUSTED MID-BOOTY BY THEIR PARENTS.

Animal Instinct

"A friend of mine was going out of town for a long weekend, so he asked me if I would mind stopping by his place and feeding his pets. I went there with my boyfriend, and, of course—empty house, two crazy kids—we ended up getting a little frisky. We were both naked, and he was just about to head down south when one of my friend's golden retrievers began sniffing around my, um, area. My guy looked over at me, and we were both so shocked at what was happening that we froze for a moment. We were about to push the dog away, except we didn't have the chance to because my friend unexpectedly came home. Apparently, there was a mix-up with the flights, and when he walked in, he saw the whole scenario! I screamed, the dog ran, and for the rest of that summer, everyone called me Scooby Snacks!" —Allison, 25

This pooch put his snout somewhere it shouldn't have been.

Good thing we can't see what's going on down below

See No Evil, Hear Some Evil

"The weekend of my friend Christine's wedding, the bridal party stayed at her parents' country estate. The best man, Steve, and I had hooked up in the past, but since we weren't dating, we couldn't ask to share a bedroom. Christine's parents ended up putting me in a room with her sister Janet, who is blind. After the rehearsal dinner, Steve and I were feeling randy, but couldn't

"After the rehearsal dinner, everyone went to bed... except the best man and me."

find a spare room. Then Steve suggested we have sex in the room I was sharing with Janet. We crept into my bed, and while Janet slept, we had slow, almost-silent sex. The next morning Janet said, 'Thanks for keeping it down last night.' When I asked her what she was talking about, she said, 'Come on, I'm blind, not deaf.'" —Melody, 26

Temptation Island

"My girlfriend and I went to Jamaica for vacation. One day we took a boat out to a little island. Since there were lots of people around, we decided to wade out into the sea to have a little frisky fun. Suddenly, we heard screams and turned to see an old lady frantically pointing at us and yelling in front of the crowd, 'Oh my goodness, those two sickos are having sex!' To make matters worse, we then had to take the boat back with the same woman." —Brian, 27

Frozen Sinners

"I was dating a guy who managed a supermarket, so we made use of his workplace after hours. We were in the frozen-food section, and I grabbed some pudding to use on him. We were totally engrossed in our messy machinations when we heard a noise. Standing there by our heap of clothes was Eldon, the 70-year-old night janitor, getting an eyeful of our naked chocolate-covered bodies." —Jen, 24

19

Talk about a compromising position

Mat required, clothing optional

Yogi Bare-All

"My boyfriend is a yoga instructor, and he convinced me to try nude yoga. One morning, we locked the door to the studio where he teaches, then stripped down to our birthday suits and started contorting ourselves into all kinds of positions. We were both in the middle of a frog-stand position when he got very turned on. I came out of my pose and started to mess around with him while he remained on his head. We were really in the moment when the door to the studio opened. It was the head yogi, who'd used his master key to get in. My boyfriend and I freaked out, but the yogi was very chill and just told us, 'Don't worry, sex and yoga go very well together.'" —Tanya, 29

The Big Zipper

"I was at my company's holiday party when my girlfriend and I started feeling frisky. We decided to creep away to the coatroom to get down to some business of our own. She was on her knees about to pleasure me when I heard someone come in. Before she could get up, my boss was standing right in front of us. To cover, she said, 'Yup, your zipper is definitely stuck, but hopefully your tailor can fix it.' I didn't think my boss would believe it, but he offered to give me the name of his tailor before walking out, so I guess it worked." —Sam, 22

44% OF GUYS ADMIT THEY'VE BEEN CAUGHT IN THE ACT.

Frisky Flick

"My girlfriend has a thing for scary movies, so I took her to a freaky slasher flick. The girls in the audience were screaming throughout the movie, and I decided to make a little game out of it. Every time I heard a squeal, I would touch my girlfriend in a naughty place. With every scream, I upped the ante. It was perfect because the noise drowned out her moans. We thought we were being so sly until an usher walked in and told us that people had been complaining about all the dirty sounds we'd been making. I turned around to see two pre-teen boys laughing their butts off." —Brendan, 22

Hand Solo

"My roommate and his friend went to play basketball one day, and I decided to do something a little more enjoyable. We didn't have any porn in the house, so I popped in *Return of the Jedi* since I've always had a Princess Leia fantasy. I was in mid-action when my roommate suddenly came back. He and his friend burst out laughing when they saw me on the couch with a pitched tent in my pants, a towel on my lap, and Luke Skywalker on the screen." —Tim, 25

This guy prefers individual sports.

"Oh, please, I did *not* need to see that!"

Twin Peaks

"My fiancé, Rick, and I took a trip home so he could meet my 8-year-old twin brother and sister. When we arrived at my family's house, we couldn't find the kids anywhere. I figured they were outside playing, so we went upstairs to rest before dinner. But when Rick spied the comfy bed from my childhood, he got this devilish look in his eyes. I knew just what he was thinking, so I stripped down to my thong and climbed into bed. He took off his clothes and

"I knew what he was thinking, so I stripped down to my thong and climbed into bed."

crawled in beside me. Things were really heating up just as my brother and sister popped up on either side of the bed and yelled 'Gotcha!' at the top of their lungs. Rick, stark naked, jumped off me and tumbled onto the floor. I started screaming at them to get out. Then, before we could get dressed, my mom came upstairs to see what all the commotion was about. Even though they are in college now, my sibs still give us hell about that afternoon." —Sheri, 31

19

These two were doing more than just holding hands.

OCCUPIED

Schoolhouse Romp

"I teach English at a high school, and last year I was asked to chaperone the prom with my girlfriend Melissa. During a slow dance, we were feeling naughty, so she took me to an out-of-the-way women's bathroom. We were fooling around in one of the stalls when all of a sudden we saw a flash. I looked up to see two of my female students leaning over the wall, taking pictures. I chased them out of the bathroom, but I couldn't exactly give them a detention, so instead, I took the film out of the camera. Rumors started surfacing the next day, but I denied them." —*Dean, 29*

"We were feeling naughty, so she took me into the women's bathroom."

Dance-Floored

"My girlfriend and I were at a local club and were having more fun than we should have. As we started gyrating to the music things got progressively slower and more intimate. Before we knew it, we were groping each other madly. We'd sequestered ourselves on the fringes of the dance floor where we thought we'd be inconspicuous, but then the deejay announced 'Will the couple getting freaky in the corner please find a room?' We slinked off like two shamed dogs, never to return." —*Andy, 24*

"As we gyrated to the music, things got more intimate. Then the deejay made an announcement...."

CAUGHT-IN-THE-ACT COMEBACKS

There's no denying what you were up to...or is there?

"Now that you mention it, that birthmark on your butt *is* shaped like North Dakota."

"Wait a minute. You're not my gynecologist!"

"It took a while, but I think I got the snake venom out of your thigh!"

"Yep, the springs on this old couch are still all right."

"And you say this workout will tone my gluteus maximus?"

"I just wanted to make sure this spatula's strong enough to handle extra-big buns....I mean, burgers."

Swinging Single

"My guy told me he had a fantasy about putting me in this sex-swing contraption that he'd seen online. I wanted to give him a surprise, so I ordered one and had it installed while he was at work. It was tricky to get into, but I followed the directions carefully, and by the time he was due home, I was naked and hanging from the living room ceiling. There was just one problem: He'd brought a couple of his work buddies home with him! My guy tried to rush them out, but they'd already seen me hanging there—and even though I was furiously trying to free myself, the unfamiliar straps and cuffs were too much for me to deal with. His friends still tease him about his 'playground'… and I avoid the company picnic!" —Kiki, 26

"Get the hell out! Can't you see we're busy?"

He got a little extra with his combo meal.

Dirty Drive-Thru

"On our way home late one night, my girlfriend and I drove to a fast-food joint to get some midnight munchies. While I was ordering, she reached over and unzipped my pants. At first I resisted, but after she trailed her fingers over my chest and stomach, I gave in. The whole time she was pleasuring me, I moaned in ecstasy. We were both smiling when we pulled up to the pickup window…and so were all the workers, who started clapping. They thanked us for making the graveyard shift more entertaining. We hadn't realized there'd been a camera aimed right at our windshield!" —Lyle, 25

A Breast Seller

"I work at a bookstore in my town with my girlfriend. After closing time one night, I pulled my girl into the closet for some ation. We messed around, but soon discovered that the door had automatically locked behind us. We had to spend the night in the closet, so we passed out par-

"We were messing around and soon discovered that the door had locked behind us."

tially clothed. The next morning, our boss found us, seminaked and cuddling. Before my girl could button her shirt, he reprimanded us and left. I thought we'd be fired, but the next day my boss left a copy of a romance novel on my desk with a note that read: 'I bet you guys could teach this author a thing or two.'" —Frank, 30

19

No grandmas allowed.

Talk about a not-so-sweet surprise

Cookie Monster

CRAZY CHICK!

"My live-in boyfriend is in the army and was sent overseas for a few months last year. One afternoon, I got horny and started pleasuring myself on the couch in the living room. We live across the street from his parents,

Ride Him, Cowgirl!

"My boyfriend and I went to visit his grandmother on her farm in Vermont for a weekend. On Saturday morning after breakfast, we were both feeling frisky, so we went back into our bedroom while his grandma went out to do chores. Well, she came back before we were finished and walked in on me straddling him. She looked horrified and immediately turned around and left. We didn't see her again until dinner, when she told me that the next time I wanted to ride something, she'd saddle up the horse for me." —Elka, 30

Yeah, she got some boot-y.

"We lived across the street from his parents, who were gone for the day, so I didn't lock the front door."

and I thought they had gone out for the day, so I didn't bother to lock the front door. One minute I was lying naked on the sofa, enjoying myself, and the next thing I knew, my boyfriend's mother was standing over me with a stunned expression on her face. She had baked cookies for me, and when no one had answered the door, she'd just let herself in. I was so embarrassed, I had no idea what to say, so I told her that I had a yeast infection and was inserting a suppository. Judging from the skeptical look on her face and the way she hightailed it out of my house, I don't think she believed me." —Jane, 32

Wild Ride

"I was on a roller coaster with my boyfriend when I got a crazy idea. I unzipped his pants and slipped my hand into his boxers, doing a little twisting and turning of my own. When we got off the ride, we passed a huge screen that flashed pictures showing each twosome on the coaster right before the major drop. When our picture popped up, my hand was clearly in my boyfriend's lap, and he had an ecstatic expression on his face. A mother reached over to pull her kid away from the screen right before we took off running."

—Shannon, 21

It's raining men!

Team Ass-Got

"Four years after our college graduation, my fiancé, Mary, and I decided to go back for the homecoming game. During the third quarter, I suggested we sneak off to the empty locker room and have sex. We must have lost track of time because all of a sudden we were interrupted by the football team returning to the locker room after the game! I jumped in front of Mary to hide her naked body, but the guys had already gotten a good peek. Then I said, 'The other team kidnapped us, stripped us, and threw us in the showers!' When the guys burst out laughing, I knew we were busted."

—Scott, 27

RAH RAH RAW!

Pom-Pom Passion

"I'm dating a guy who is in his 40s and has a 17-year-old son. My sweetie was feeling bummed about getting older, so one night when his kid was out with his friends, I devised a plan to perk him up. I brought over my old cheerleading outfit and started to perform the cheers I did back in high school, giving them a naughty spin. Between each cheer, I'd do cartwheels and high kicks, letting him get a peek of me sans panties. Then I would strip away one item of his clothing before going on to the next set. With each 'Rah-rah-ree, bend me over your knee!' and 'Sis-boom-bang, do you want to see my thang?' I could see him getting more excited. When I could tell he was as hot as an 18-year-old jock, I straddled him on the couch. There we were, my stud butt naked

> ## "Between each cheer, I'd do high kicks, letting him get a peek of me sans panties."

with me on top, bouncing all around on the springy couch, when his son came in with his friends in tow. My boyfriend and I froze, and his son made an immediate retreat out the door…but not before one of his pals said, 'Wow, your dad's so cool. He's getting it on with a cheerleader!'"

—Leslie, 28

19

"Face it, girl.
No matter what
you wear, I'll
always be hotter."

OUTRAGEOUSLY EVIL INSULTS

These chicks survived a verbal thrashing so fierce, they're still licking their wounds. Read on and prepare to be shocked.

Party Smarty-Pants

"I attended a shindig with one of my coworkers, and the guy she'd been trying to set me up with for months was there. My friend made sure we wound up talking, and I was happy to find that Mark and I had a lot in common: We liked the same music, drove the same kind of car, and laughed at the same things. As the evening was winding down, I made a casual suggestion that we exchange numbers. Mark looked at me in shock and said, 'I only go out with people who are capable of providing a little more intellectual stimulation.' Hello! I thought we were supposed to be making small talk. He made me feel like an idiot. I just smiled, said, 'Oh, I understand,' and left, completely humiliated. My friend has since disowned Mark for his behavior and vowed never to set me up again."—*Elaine, 32*

Slim Pick-Ons

"I am about 6 feet tall and weigh 125 pounds—I've always been naturally tall and thin. I know that people think I have an eating disorder, but I don't—it's just my genes. One day, a woman came into the bank where I work, looked me dead in the eye, and said, 'You think that starving yourself will make you beautiful, but people like you can never be skinny enough. If you had any idea how ugly you really are, you'd be sick.' For the rest of the day, I felt like a bony freak of nature."
—*Marielle, 18*

20

Size Queen

"I was at an exclusive boutique when I found the perfect skirt to wear to an upcoming wedding. But when I came out of the dressing room, the woman working there said, 'Hmmm. You could really use a bigger size.' The medium I had on looked and felt okay to me, but to humor her, I asked if she had a large. She did—not only was it

"When I came out of the dressing room, the woman helping me said, 'Hmmm. You could really use a bigger size.'"

Medium!

After what happened to her, she was dressed to kill.

baggy on me, but it was in an unflattering color. I told her I would take the medium, explaining that I was bloated from my period, but it would fit perfectly later in the month. She said, 'Sorry, but I'm the owner, and I'm not selling you that skirt. Having someone with hips like yours wearing my clothes is just bad advertising for me.' I was so pissed off that I stormed out of the store—and right into another boutique down the street. There, I bought a similar skirt—in a medium!" —Suzanne, 28

"You wax my privates, I'll wax yours."

Hair-Raising Experience

"It was my first time getting a bikini wax. I was self-conscious about being so near-naked in front of someone—especially in the unshaven state I'd heard was necessary for a good wax. I went to a fancy place, thinking that they would be more likely to make an effort to help their clients feel comfortable. But after I pulled on the paper panties, hopped on the table, and let the aesthetician smear wax on my thigh, she sighed and said, 'You're extremely hairy. You are young, so you should be able to show off your body without worrying about looking like a man. You really need electrolysis to take care of this problem.' I mumbled, 'No, thanks,' let her finish the waxing, and then bolted out feeling like the ape woman from a circus freak show." —Michelle, 22

OUTRAGEOUS RETORTS

"HEY, I CAN LOSE WEIGHT, BUT YOU'LL STILL BE UGLY."

"OH WOW, YOUR PARENTS MUST NOT LOVE YOU, HUH?"

"GEE, WHEN'S THE LAST TIME YOU GOT ANY ACTION?"

Pregnant Pause

"After going through a really stressful time in my life, I put on a few pounds. I felt pretty lousy about myself, but I was trying my best to take off the weight. One summer Saturday afternoon, I was hanging out with my best friend. We went out for a nice lunch and then hit a few stores for some shopping. We were on the elevator in a department store, heading for the shoe sale, when it stopped on the third floor and another woman stepped in. She pushed the button for her floor, looked me up and down for a minute, and then asked me, 'When is the baby due?' Ummm, I wasn't pregnant."

—Melanie, 29

"Get back here, bitch, so I can wipe that smile off your face."

Some morons just love to mouth off.

Sore Loser

"I was self-conscious on my first day of college because I had a small cold sore on my lip. It was almost healed, and I managed to convince myself that nobody would notice it. That afternoon, we had a dormitory meeting and everyone had to go around and introduce themselves. I was happy to see that there were a bunch of cute guys that I would be sharing space with for the next year, and I vowed to make a good first impression on them. So when my turn came, I gave a big smile and said, 'Hi, my name is Kelly. I'm from Florida, and I'm really glad to be here.' Everyone murmured hello, except for one freak who said, 'Hey, what's that thing on your lip? Herpes? Watch out, everyone, she's contagious!' I tried to laugh it off, but, of course, I was so livid, I could've killed him."

—Kelly, 21

See-Through Slam

"A few months ago at work, I wore a really pretty summery dress that was ever-so-slightly transparent. A snarky coworker was walking behind me down the hall, and she said really loudly so that everyone around could hear, 'Honey, I'm thinking you could use a thong with that!' I was so upset, I had to borrow a sweater from my cubemate to tie around my waist." —Jenny, 25

"I was wearing a slightly transparent dress when a coworker said...."

No Thanks for the Mammaries

"I was helping to clean up after Thanksgiving dinner and chatting with my man's mom. His sister had been there with her bratty baby, and I said something about how well the baby was doing with his switch to solid foods. His mom said, 'Yes, she's a wonderful mother. It's too bad you won't be able to breast-feed like she does.' I said, 'What do you mean?' and she said, 'Well, look at those teeny things. How on earth could you squeeze enough out of there to nourish a child?'" —*Betty, 28*

Despite what his mom says, bigger isn't always better.

"When I told my coworker that I was bringing my guy to the party, she said the rudest thing."

Stud Snub

"My boss is known for his huge Labor Day parties. A coworker who has the same title I do but is more buddy-buddy with the boss came up to me that week and said, 'Are you bringing your boyfriend to the party?' I told her that I hadn't even thought about bringing a guest, and she said, 'Well, my husband's invited, but that's because the boss wants good-looking guys there. So I wouldn't even ask about your boyfriend.' Before I could even react to her, she trotted back to her office." —*Jan, 28*

Big-Nose Blunder

"One day in cosmetology school we had a guest speaker from a swanky salon. She asked for a volunteer for a haircut demonstration, and I raised my hand. She pulled my hair back and asked the other students what they noticed about me. While everyone shouted out 'round face,' and 'angular features,' one person in the back said, 'huge-ola nose.' At that the speaker said, 'Yeah, you do have a schnoz,' and based the rest of her lecture on how to use a hairstyle to mask a client's worst feature." —*Carrie, 27*

HOW TO...
HANDLE A SLAM
Simple ways to stay sane when you've been shafted.

Defuse the Fight

Try to steer things back to civility by saying "Are you sure you meant that?" or "Wait a minute, let's start over." That'll cool both of your tempers before you start spewing evil words of your own at her.

Draw the Line

When a comment crosses into the personal zone, make it clear right away that it's out of line and you want to change the subject. Say something like, "You know what? You're taking it too far. Seriously, stop."

Go Over Her Head

If you find yourself being dissed by a bitchy salesperson, calmly ask to speak to her manager or supervisor. That'll shut her up quick. Plus, a higher-up is more equipped to deal with your issue anyway.

SOURCE: SAM HORN, COMMUNICATION EXPERT AND AUTHOR OF *TAKE THE BULLY BY THE HORNS*

Too bad every rose has its thorns

This chick doesn't take crap from anybody.

Birthday Bash

"It was my 25th birthday, and my boyfriend had made plans for a romantic dinner. That afternoon he'd sent me a gorgeous bouquet of roses at work. I was in the best mood as I left my office with the flowers in my arms to go meet him. But as I walked down the side-walk to the subway, a guy came up to me, said, 'Pretty flowers, ugly girl,' and just kept on walking. I was so crushed, but, luckily, my sweet boyfriend told me I was the most beautiful woman in the world."

—Andrea, 25

Catty Comparathon

"I was dating a guy whose mom always found ways to bring up his ex: 'That sunset makes me think of the orange shirt Wendy always used to wear!' 'I wish Wendy were here; she'd remember how that song went!' Finally, my guy-said something to his mom. Sure enough, the next time I saw her she said, 'I know I'm not supposed to bring her up, but Wendy just loved my gravy!'"

—Jacqui, 29

Creepy Compliment

"I was interviewing for a new job, so I had my hair blown out and wore a nice dress on the day of the interview. I looked good, but not that different from my normal work appearance. After a staff meeting, a guy from

"At our staff meeting, this guy said, 'Wow, you look really nice today.' Then he dropped the bomb...."

another department said, 'Wow, you look really nice today.' I was flattered, so I thanked him and was about to walk away when he added, 'Because when you started working here, we all talked about how skanky you looked. It's about time you pulled yourself together.' What an ass!" —Kalenna, 28

20

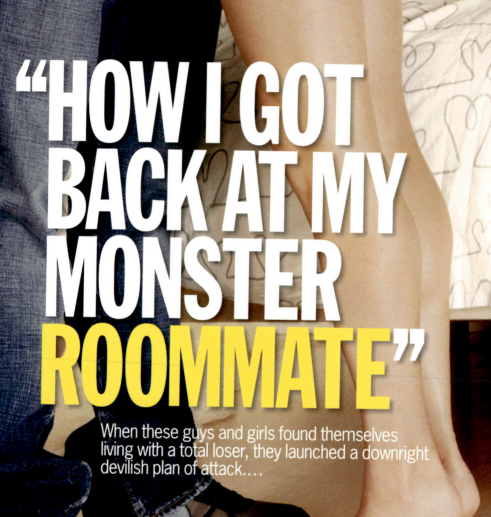

"HOW I GOT BACK AT MY MONSTER ROOMMATE"

When these guys and girls found themselves living with a total loser, they launched a downright devilish plan of attack....

"I said he could borrow my shampoo, *not* my girlfriend."

Houseguest From Hell

"When my friend got evicted from his apartment, I offered to let him stay at my place briefly. Well, he ended up staying for months. The bills started to add up, and he kept making excuses for why he couldn't pay. Meanwhile, every week, he'd come home with a new toy like a TV or stereo. Finally, I got so fed up that I had a friend break into the apartment and steal his expensive stuff (and mine, to make it look more legit). After he sold the loot for me, I made enough money to finally cover my bills. My roommate, thinking I lived in a bad neighborhood, decided to move out." —*Michael, 24*

One for the Record

"When I was in med school, I had an obnoxious roommate who had a girlfriend, but still brought home other girls. He always made a lot of noise just so I would know what was going on in his bedroom. I told him to keep it down, especially while I was studying, but he refused. So one night, when I knew he was out scoping for women, I slipped a voice-activated recorder under his bed. The next day when I played it back, I heard my roommate with another woman. Then I mailed the tape to his girlfriend. The chick dumped him, and I found a new place a few days after." –*Taylor, 32*

21

Porky the Pig

"I lived with this girl who was obsessed with bacon. She would microwave an entire plate of it, then leave it out on the counter and pick at it throughout the day. She was also a slob and a cheapo who never paid the rent on time. We all couldn't stand her, but felt badly about kicking her out. One afternoon, a bunch of us were cleaning without her help. As I was scraping grease off the stove, I noticed that it looked like burnt bacon bits. So I scooped up the nasty scum and put it on top of her plate of pork product." —Tanya, 31

If it was your turn to do the dishes, you'd be PO'd too.

Whipping Boy

"A few years ago, I had a roommate who took my stuff without asking, ate the food in the fridge, and constantly left the place a wreck. I was finally able to get back at him when I found out that he had a big interview with a law firm coming up later in the week. The morning of the interview, I woke up early and filled the pockets of his only suit with whipped cream. Then I went through his briefcase and wrote 'Will work for food' on his résumé. When I came home that night, he was absolutely furious, and he moved out two days later." —Zach, 27

KEEP IT DOWN! WHAT'S THE MOST COMMON COMPLAINT AMONG ROOMIES? ACCORDING TO THERAPIST SUSAN FEE, AUTHOR OF *MY ROOMMATE IS DRIVING ME CRAZY*, IT'S HEARING THE PERSON THEY LIVE WITH HAVING SEX.

"I put on a leather catsuit and walked in on my roommate and her boyfriend...."

Puss in Boots

"After relocating to Atlanta, I shared an apartment with this girl named Becky. During the day, she would get busy with her boyfriend in the living room. I got so sick of her heinous behavior that I devised a plan. The next time she and her boyfriend started going at it on the couch, I put on a leather catsuit I'd worn for Halloween, strapped on knee-high black boots, walked in on them, and asked, 'Hey, Becky, do you mind if I join in?' My roommate and her boyfriend never did it outside of the bedroom again." —Sharon, 26

Pumpin' Her Up

"I lived with this girl who happened to be a personal trainer. Maggie was in ridiculously good shape and was constantly pointing out that I was flabby and needed to work out. I'd never had body-image issues before, but after living with her for just a few months, I felt fat. I asked her to back off, but then she just gave me critical looks. Finally, I'd had enough of her judgments, so I replaced her protein-shake powder with a weight-gaining supplement. Since she worked out so much, she started getting huge muscles and looked like a female body-builder. By the time she bought a new container of protein powder, I'd already found another apartment." —*Carla, 30*

Our advice: Stop pulling out your hair and start looking for a new pad.

THE WORLD'S WORST ROOMMATE OFFENSES

If your roomie pulls one of these moves, start plotting your payback.

Eating your Ben & Jerry's while you're away and replacing it with fat-free sorbet

Leaving a butt imprint on the kitchen counter after a session with her boyfriend

Clipping her cat's toenails with your personal nail clipper

Using your favorite and very expensive little black dress as part of her costume for a pimp and ho–themed Halloween party

Room-Mating Call

"In college, my roomie and I lived in a studio with two twin beds. So whenever her boyfriend stayed over, I crashed at a friend's dorm. Eventually I got so peeved about it that I told her she needed to find a different place to shack up with him. Well, two nights later, they started going at it just a few feet away from me! The next morning, my roommate got up and left for class. I was still pretty annoyed, so when I saw her hot boyfriend sleeping in nothing but his boxers, I put the moves on him. He woke up, and we fooled around before my roommate came back." —*Shara, 22*

Some roomies share *everything.*

21

Even celebrities do dumb things.

STARS FESS UP TO COSMO

Normally, A-listers pay a bevy of publicists to cover up their scandalous secrets, but we got them to spill their dirty deeds and totally embarrassing blunders.

Kate Hudson

"I would call a guy, and if he didn't pick up, I'd hang up a thousand times on his answering machine. We have all done that, right? I also used to do drive-bys… drive by a guy's house while crouching down so he can't see you."

Ben Stiller

"I came back to L.A., sneaked into Christine [Taylor's] house, and filled it with flowers and candles. When she walked in, I got down on one knee, then realized I'd left the ring in my backpack in the other room."

Brittany Murphy

"The worst thing I did was look inside a closet in an ex-boyfriend's house. I was looking for something, so I opened up the door, and it was a closet of ex-girlfriends. All the mementos, journals, love letters, everything. I was like, 'Aaahhh!'"

Minnie Driver

"I was 16 and madly in love with this guy. He wouldn't speak to me, though, so I enrolled as the model in his art class and he had to look at me for five hours every day. He would always draw me with a really big ass and really big thighs."

Matt Damon

"Brad [Pitt] was sitting in his car, and George [Clooney] tapped the car and said, 'All right, take care.' When he pulled his hand away, he'd left a bumper sticker that read 'Small Penis Onboard.' So Brad drove through rush-hour traffic with it, and all these people were looking and waving."

Rebecca Romijn

"My last night of shooting *X-Men*, I did a celebratory shot of tequila with the people from special effects, and that, combined with the paint I'd been breathing all day long, made me sick. I vomited blue…so gross!"

Poppy Montgomery

"My dates always turn into bad romantic comedies. I'm incredibly clumsy. Once, I lit a napkin on fire while reaching for the breadbasket. I was so busy talking, I didn't even notice."

Ryan Reynolds

"When I was in ninth grade, five friends and I picked up a math teacher's Volkswagen Bug and hid it a block away. Afterward, I heard that moving a car more than 10 feet qualifies as grand theft auto, so I could have gotten in big trouble."

22

Published in 2006 by Hearst Books
A Division of Sterling Publishing Co., Inc.
387 Park Avenue South, New York, NY 10016

Library of Congress Cataloging-in-Publication Data

Cosmo confessions / from the editors of Cosmopolitan.
p. cm.
ISBN-13: 978-158816-467-4
ISBN-10: 1-58816-467-5
1. Man-woman relationships--Anecdotes. 2. Dating (social customs)--Anecdotes. 3. Sex--Anecdotes.
4. Sex--customs--Anecdotes. 5. Single women--Anecdotes. 6. Single men--Anecdotes. I. Cosmopolitan (New York, N.Y. : 1952)
HQ801.C729 2006
306.73--dc22 2005056258

10 9 8 7 6 5 4 3 2 1

COSMOPOLITAN

Editor-in-Chief Kate White
Design Director Ann P. Kwong
Edited by John Searles
Book Design by Peter Perron
Senior Editor Jennifer Benjamin

cosmopolitan.com

For information about custom editions, special sales, premium and corporate purchases, please contact Sterling Special Sales Department at 800-805-5489 or specialsales@sterlingpub.com.

Distributed in Canada by Sterling Publishing
c/o Canadian Manda Group, 165 Dufferin Street
Toronto, Ontario, Canada M6K 3H6

Distributed in Australia by Capricorn Link (Australia) Pty. Ltd.
P.O. Box 704, Windsor, NSW 2756 Australia

Manufactured in China

ISBN-13: 978-158816-467-4
ISBN-10: 1-58816-467-5